BLUEPRINT
FOR AN ARTIST

*A personal account — a memoir of sorts.
How one artist can reach out and point the way for another:
by generosity of spirit and deed and by example.*

HEATHER GAIL HARMAN

Published by:
Heather Gail Harman

Blueprint for an Artist
Copyright 2018 by Heather Gail Harman
heatherandwill@hotmail.com

All artwork by Heather Gail Harman
Photos as credited

Many thanks to Paul de Noya for permission to quote him!

Cover image "Into The Void" is a work in progress adapted from an original photo reference Getty Images - copyright secured. It is forbidden to reproduce the image in any form. More information about the publication of a limited edition print run will be found on heatherharmanartist.com in early 2019.

All rights reserved. Without limiting the rights under copyright reserved above, no part of this publication may be reproduced, stored in or introduced into a retrieval system, or transmitted, in any form, or by any means (electronic, mechanical, photocopying, recording, or otherwise) without the prior written permission of both the copyright owner and the above publisher of this book.

'A man's work is nothing but this slow trek to rediscover through the detours of art, those two or three great and simple images in whose presence his heart first opened.'
Albert Camus

This memoire is dedicated to my friends, Lynne Goodall and Maisie Van Courtland, who kept the faith when it mattered, and over the years continually convinced various managements that a great artist should never be ignored, and there would always be a massive interest in his life and work.

This is also for the loyal Scott followers. The internet has now made it so easy to keep track of his career and to meet each other online. A good many managed to stay in touch via telephone and snail mail all along and I have promised to write this story to many of them on a few occasions, and I have finally done so. Back in the 70s and 80s we would talk about the possibility of Scott's music being appreciated by a whole new audience worldwide; a younger audience who would access the music on their terms. That started to happen before the internet and has grown massively since. This book is for you too.

Finally for Scott and for his family, and for my family who will not be surprised I have finally got around to it.

PREFACE

WHY HAVE I CALLED THIS ACCOUNT 'BLUEPRINT FOR AN ARTIST'?

I have grown up knowing that pure chance; happenstance has had a massive influence over my life.

For some years now this account has been promised to those who know me, and other artists. But for me it is a bit like having teeth pulled. I would rather write about someone else's life than my own. It isn't comfortable, but it is also for my Granddaughter, Thorie, but more than anything this is also for a community of wonderful people I have met on Facebook who are keen followers of the subject of this memoire.

Artists grow and develop in many ways, and my path has been clear to track. The signposts were astoundingly clear, because I was lucky, really lucky, in that in some way the stars collided and one person inspired my creative existence. And it matters, because without being over emotional about this, without this one person, I would not be who I am, and maybe not even doing what I do. Who knows? But the odds were against it.

A few people can say that. Artists have always inspired artists. Others have been so inspired and influenced, but I know that history will tell the story of an extraordinary artist, and I was lucky enough to be around at the time. I have lived for 50 years knowing how extraordinary a talent he is; always was and remains; so much so that now, in his 70's, his career is growing and International respect has grown with it. There is hardly a popular musician, that doesn't revere him. But for so long it was thought that would not be the case.

This is a story which begins in the fantastic and influential 1960's. I am a 'working class' girl from the Industrial Midlands in the UK. No artists in my family, no one who had been to college or university in my family. No 'role models' and above all no real idea of what an 'artist', really was. Now 50 years later, I am still aware of the fact that is some way 'fate' took a part, or just pure luck; I don't have a name for it, but I sure am grateful for it. I am now a well-respected authority in my specialism in Fine Art; a painter, an author, a tutor, a mentor and an historian of my medium. I live the life of an artist in total control of my artistic creativity and destiny.

Artistic freedom is a lot to do with why I am writing this.

But I have roots, a beginning: and a vital part of the jigsaw puzzle that makes up my story is due to a young guy from the USA, who did not come from anything like my background. I mean chalk and cheese. He grew up in Hollywood and because of his amazing talent, was lauded and applauded as a young child and into his teenage years, on a nationwide stage.

He stretched my mind and my imagination. He showed me what being an artist was and in a world full of hype and 'pop' stars, this guy was the real deal.

But this story will be difficult to write. Part of this story has got to be written by the young teenager I was in the 60's, but the greater part is written by me, a successful artist with a wonderful career. Identity is complicated, but self-knowledge over a period of years is so valuable and humbling in equal measure.

Heather Gail Harman,
Spain 2018

CAREER NUMBER ONE

THE SWINGING 60's.
A VERY MAGICAL TIME
TO BE A TEENAGER.

There is an age old statement; 'Artists are born—not made'. Well this book will go some way to examine that statement, in an attempt to come to some personal conclusions and also to open up the debate a little, so that other artists might recognize some of the feelings and emotions that were my building blocks along the way.

Artists tend to question themselves on many different levels:

- 'Am I good Enough?', a common one.
- 'Can I be a Professional?'
- 'Am I being taken seriously?',
- 'Can I earn my living creating art?'

Add to that:

- 'Is there any point in my trying?'
- 'Is anything I am doing important enough to be a good influence over other artists who will follow?'

So many questions and many of them getting in the way of creating and growing.

After hearing a statement made by musician Midge Ure, who was interviewed following David Bowie's death, he said something which struck a chord with me. Talking about Bowie, Midge said:

'It is not very often you get to meet your heroes. And it is not very often if you do meet them that you are actually quite pleased you did meet them'.

I have indeed met a lot of famous names in my life. I get what Midge meant.

Not to be let down by our idols is a biggie. A real biggie. The prospect of meeting someone you idolise for whatever reason, and being disappointed with them as a person, is enough to stop many people from meeting and shaking hands with their idols; given they were lucky enough to have the chance to do so. Frankly for me as a young artist, it was a massive risk to take. It is ironic however, that my idol faced the same challenges in his most successful early years and decided he didn't want to meet a man who had been the major musical influence over his career. Such is the fear of disappointment or just the 'fear' itself.

How it all began

On my website (www.heatherharmanartist.com) there is a pretty comprehensive biography page and so there is no point my repeating the facts and logistics of my career here. Suffice to say that I have been enjoying a wonderful professional career now for over 40 years, worked for and with many known names, and now, I am considered to be a Pastel medium specialist.

But I have in fact had two careers and both as an artist.

So, I was artistically 'born' and I remember the day it happened.

I had a pretty poor childhood health wise. I don't think there were many illness's I didn't have at one point or another, and I was always off school, laid up on the sofa in the lounge being fed homemade soup. So I couldn't read and write until I was eight years old. But, I could draw and listen to music. I could also crochet and knit and embroider; just about anything I turned my hands to I could do, thanks to my Grandmother who taught me everything. She was a clever lady who was forced to sacrifice her dream of being a professional pianist so that she could look after the family. That is what good working class girls did. They got a job and helped Mum and Dad raise the siblings. She had me knitting baby clothes by the age of six; reading knitting patterns and even designing a few before I was ten.

But my passion was for two things which for me were inseparable even as a young child; music and drawing and painting. They were my friends. I loved my colouring books, and different kinds of crayons. I can shut my eyes and smell colouring books and crayons now. The smell I recall reminds me of being laid up on the sofa ill. My 'familiar' world.

I had 'real' friends but was always catching up on school stuff and to be honest, I was quite happy with my own company. Then I could draw and listen to music. Bliss.

Then came The Beatles — Oh Yeah Yeah Yeah!

Fast forward a couple of years and the Beatles had arrived, and so had Radio Luxemburg and Radio's Caroline and London. I was eleven years old, and remember now the first time I saw the Beatles and my family's reaction to them. I was a fan of course; it seemed every teenager was and thinking about it all, what a great time to become a teenager the mid 60's were: especially for a music fan.

One thing is for sure, the 60's wouldn't have been the 60's without the Beatles. The music industry was changed forever because of them. I was thirteen, and fresh out of a two week hospital visit in early 1965. A bad dose of Glandular fever and quite a few weeks (12 to be exact) of rest and recuperation at home and doing what? Drawing and listening to music!

Drawing what? Anything. I liked Cher's clothes and drew them a lot. Flowers, jugs, figures I would copy out of books; anything that I could turn into a drawing.

I had a fabulous old Bacolite radio with strange and romantic sounding names on it like 'Hilversum', and 'Dogger', 'Paris', 'Vienna', and it tuned in to every part of the world. It was a pretty large radio and covered the top of our sideboard. I found Radio London about a week after its first transmission. It was so unheard of I thought no one but me knew about it. I remember the first Kenny Everett transmission.

When I went to bed it was to listen to Radio Luxemburg in the hope of hearing my favourite Phil Spectre produced music. I used to dream of growing up to be a female Phil Spectre, with a mass of mixers and control panels around me! I always did have a good imagination.

I was a 60's girl in every way. I had a great *stereo* record player (important that—it being stereo!) and a great selection of LP's; mainly musicals and Elvis and of course the Beatles, and a couple of Shirley Bassey albums too. My Grandmother took me to see her live a couple of times when I was eleven years old. I had albums; more albums than my girlfriends, and that '*stereo*' record player was the source of great pride to me. (Though I later found out it took my family six months to pay for it. It evidently was a very good record player). There was 'Top of the Pops' of course, and 'Ready Steady Go', 'Thank You Lucky Stars' on a Saturday night, also Juke Box Jury on around teatime Saturday.

Did I have any thoughts of a career, or what I wanted to do when I grew up? Well apart from the pipe dream of being the female Phil Spectre? No I didn't. Professional ambition didn't really exist in my family, where getting married, becoming a nurse or a teacher, or getting a job in a shop was the norm.

But a Change was Gonna Come

February 17, 1965 became a date to remember for me. Three guys, musicians arrived in the UK from California.

My days would rarely change: Surf the radio most of the day and 'tape' (on my Grundig TK45 reel to reel tape recorder) which I had been given for Christmas. I would record any song that I loved on the Pirate stations.

Then I heard a song that stopped me in my tracks.

I didn't even think to press the record button. I remember staring at my radio, and all I could think of all day was that song coming on the radio again so I could tape it, which it did later in the day and I still have that original crackly recording from Radio London in early 1965 to this day. A magnificent and unique voice, and a fabulous Phil Spectre like production. It was something special; totally different and as far away from anything I had heard than you could get. I played my tape recording all day and every day. 'You've Lost that Loving Feeling' was a big hit around that time, but this voice was different.

The following week, I turned on the TV for 'The Five O'Clock Club', a teenage magazine type programme presented by Muriel Young. There was that voice. I couldn't believe it. I was drawing at the time, doodling more like it, and I sat stock still. The black and white television screen was filled with the most beautiful angelic face I had ever seen; even more amazingly, the source of that great magnificent voice. Above all that voice.

It was one of those moments when time seemed to stand still. Such a powerfully rich deep voice and the face of an angel framed with long blond hair. It seemed a mismatch of voice and face, but a double whammy for sure. A potent mix for any thirteen year old girl., and right now as I write this, I am that 13 years old girl again. Some 50 years later, I can shut my eyes and I am back in that moment.

In so many ways the moment my artistic identity was born.

During that song I was scribbling a face. I HAD to. There was no video back then and no way of recording anything off the television. I might never see that face again so I drew it. I had never even considered drawing a face before. Truly for me, the face that launched an art career. I had to capture that face somehow. A pencil was all I needed.

That moment in time remains today as singularly the most important inspirational moment in my life. A significant turning point.

Could it have been any face or voice? Well you might say yes of course it would eventually have been something or someone else who would have lit a spark inside me. Maybe. But the answer is no as has been proven since, this was no ordinary pop star; no ordinary talent, no 'ordinary' anything. Quite the opposite in fact, as his increased artistic standing in the music world 50 years later has proven.

Moments like that have proved to be rare in my life; as in many people's lives I suspect. The song was 'Love Her'. The singer Scott Walker (Engel) lead singer with the Walker Brothers; an American threesome who have travelled to the UK in February 1965 in the hope of becoming successful in the exciting UK music scene. Well they did; and how.

My parents always used to say that my life changed at that time. Well I became deeply and passionately involved with my new love of portrait drawing. I was motivated. Driven even. Eyes noses lips were all of a sudden fascinating.

I started to collect pop magazines featuring articles about the Walker Brothers and of course, photographs. Now I could really practice my portrait drawing. My proud but bemused parents showed them to everyone they could, and they were impressed;

'How old is she? Thirteen? Wow. Where did that talent come from? 'She must be born an artist!

I heard that a lot of course.

'You can't teach that kind of talent. She must have been born with it'.

I really didn't care one way or another. I had my muse.

But it had begun, that persistent search for 'Where did it come from'? That talent? It must have come from somewhere. Members of my family had no idea. My parents knew, but there was little point in my telling anyone it came from Scott Walker, but as far as I was concerned it did. No one in my family drew that is for sure. I just did what I did. How good or bad it was I didn't know.

But what is obvious to now, having seen creativity sparked in others for many years, is the fact that a creative spirit, needs a 'muse'. How many young children are similarly creative and go through life without their imaginations being so captured? (How many major Music icons can trace their original muse to Elvis? Probably hundreds). For me it was a gift without measure; and to this day I encourage youngsters to draw whatever or whoever it is, that is their fascination and preoccupation. If a young football fan loves Beckham, and they want to draw him, encourage it. Genuine admiration is an important part of how a portrait painter should interact with their subjects! I know portrait painters with great reputations, who don't actually like people, or interacting with them. So why bother? (Now that is a whole different book; this one is about artistic integrity)

For me though, music and my creative art are intrinsically fused together.

The rest of my thirteenth year was spent drawing. I had my frustrations, but overall I was getting results and each success fired me up for more. There was nothing available as a source of tuition, not even books. Just my determination to improve. A lot of my artist students will recognise that.

I followed the careers of the Walker Brothers throughout and watched as they rose in stardom in the UK to rival the popularity of the Beatles. Their live shows were legend. Not just concerts, more like 'events'. I saw them in Blackpool in the summer of 1965 on the North Pier and getting them on and off the pier was like an SAS operation. I learnt early on that live Walker Brothers concerts were potentially dangerous places to be; but they were unforgettable, 60's moments, and I wouldn't have missed any one of them.

My Walker Brothers Portraits

They had massive hits (Make it Easy on Yourself, My Ship is coming in. The Sun Ain't Gonna Shine Anymore.) By the Spring on 1966, I was 14 and had produced three portraits of John Scott and Gary that I could live with. I was my own worst critic even then. Artists are never satisfied with what they produce, it is what drives them on to achieve more. They were large, full life size, moody and dramatic portraits. All pencil on white card. I never had any real art equipment then.

Then a surprise: That is putting it lightly. I was given the opportunity to take my portraits and meet the Walker Brothers who were opening a Disci Record Shop in Bletchley. Yes ok, I thought, I will believe that when it happens. At that point it was a little like meeting the Beatles, no less, and I went along with little hope of any meeting taking place

But no one reckoned on my father's emerging talents in the promotion of his artistic daughter. I went to Bletchley with my father and two friends expecting nothing. But we ended up in the shop which was a surprise. It was chaos, and the large plate glass window in the front of the store was in danger of being broken so those of us in the shop were moved to the back room, whilst the Police called for backup. Only Gary Leeds was there, the drummer with the group and a lovely guy he was too. No Scott Engel and no John Maus (Walker was their stage name). But it was chaos all the same. Not least of all because those outside didn't know that only Gary was there. So we were under siege.

Stuck in the back stock room with Gary and his minders, whilst the police did their best to protect the safety of the shop window, we were talking about my portraits and posing for local press. He was so sorry Scott was not there to see them because as the music world knew by then, Scott was an artist himself. Gary laughed almost all afternoon when my father called me 'pet'. He thought it was real 'weird man'. Evidently a very strange thing to call your daughter in the USA. When Gary left it was 'Bye Pet!'.

A Strange Place for the Portraits to be

My three portraits were eventually in the hands of the Mayor of Rugby. The local press had covered them and he wanted to hang them in the Town Hall. A couple of the councillors refused to let them be hung in the Town Hall, and the Mayor insisted that they were. The press have always loved a bit of controversy. Then came a message. The Daily Mirror wanted me, the portraits, and the Mayor for a photo shoot in the Major's Parlour in the Town Hall, at 10pm one evening. I was to be in the paper the following day hence the rush. Wow.

The Daily Mirror (August 16th 1966) I couldn't believe it. I was in a bit of a fog to be honest.

It was a different world back then being in the National press or on TV was enormous; particularly so for a young Midland teenager from an ordinary working class background.

We were met at the Mayor's office by the two reporter photographers who 'sent through' photographs to the London Mirror HQ by telephone. Smart black suits and a range of equipment, and I have always enjoyed watching professionals at work. So photos were taken and the following morning I was a Page Three Girl! (For non UK readers, the joke being the Page three of the Daily Mirror eventually became notorious for topless images of women).

Of course going to school became a whole different experience. Now I was a mini celebrity in my home town. Dubbed the 'Rugby Artist', the local press and other regional press offices picked up on the story. The BBC TV covered it too. I wish I had the footage today. The influence of the National Press meant that the portraits were eventually hung in the Rugby Town Hall, where the BBC went to film them for the news.

After Daily Mirror coverage I received a post card. It was headed ' Dear 'Pet' Heather', and I was thrilled to think that Gary of the Walker Brothers had sent me a card. All the address said was, Heather Johnston, Bath Street, Rugby. No house number, no postcodes back then. That was all that had been included in the article in the Mirror, and thinking about it, I was lucky to have received it at all. Post cards were still widely used in the 60's, but of course the signature of who wrote it was there for all to see. The signature was a pseudonym a pretty well-known one in Walker Brothers circles as I was to learn. What intrigued me were the words which seemed strange words for Gary to say, but I was nonetheless thrilled. My father read it and grinned at the 'pet' Heather. The words were beautiful and clearly heartfelt. But Dad thought Gary must have been drunk when he wrote it judging by the handwriting!

But that morning we didn't realise that it wasn't Gary that had sent it.

Scott Walker—my muse

He was of course my 'beginning', and as such is someone who I have always followed throughout his extraordinary career; through all the 'ups' and the all too prevalent 'downs'. Some of us followed during those downs, with no internet help back then. Scott was massively respected by other musicians in particular and the music industry generally. He was also the subject of quite a bit of professional jealousy as I remember. This was no ordinary pop star; Scott Engel was deeply involved with European culture, film, philosophy, art, and of course music of all variations (which I craved), and literature (another love of mine). An intellectual by any standards, all of which made me a massive fan. Frankly I was attracted to boys who wore glasses! I was reading Dostoevsky's 'The Idiot' when I was 15, along with Sartre and Camus; because of his influence (yes thanks for that Scott!)

So there was his voice, and his face ('my') face, and now a source of education in aspects of the arts I would never have known. A greater 'educational mentor' I could not have found; and the odds against a 13 year old budding artist in Rugby having someone the creative and intellectual calibre of Scott Engel cross my path were beyond low.

Paul de Noya's great article on Scott in the year 2000 explains it beautifully thus:

> The fans were not only screamers, though. There was another streak to Scott's appeal: a kind of student chic that was big among sensitive sixth-formers. They'd read his Record Mirror interviews and rush to look up "existentialist". The writer Peter York has dubbed Scott the ultimate Neurotic

Boy Outsider. He was, said York, "someone who got the style *exactly* right... He wore his shades perpetually and he was very thin. It goes without saying that he was often found in extremely low moods wandering around and worrying about something too big to explain." Suburban girls found this to be irresistible. Suburban boys made lame attempts to copy it, with horrible results. (**A profile of the fabulous Scott Walker, written for *GQ* magazine, July 2000.**)

Interesting the emphasis on 'cool" in this quote, but 'cool' it seems, is a male pre-occupation. But yes that was me to a tee. I wasn't in the 6th from when I looked up Existentialist. I was fourteen going on 15. At school I was reading Jane Austin's Emma; but at home I was reading Dostoevsky and Sartre.

The main gift I 'took' from him was an introduction to some great songwriters and composers; Tim Hardin, Michel le Grande, the fabulous Randy Newman, and his then beloved Jacques Brel. Not to mention his love of the classical. (I later produced a full exhibition of portraits of 36 of those major musical creatives and writers.)

Then there were his own iconic compositions. No longer just a singer who knew great songs, and knew how to sing them; he was now a writer of songs, and they were no ordinary songs. Was there a limit to his creativity? (Well today of course his new audience are asking the same questions). He was producing work in the UK which may have started out as heavily influenced initially by Phil Spectre, (having crossed paths with the Spectre in the US prior to moving to the UK) but he was his own artist that was for sure. A complex and creative character, as Paul De Noyer describes:

> ... Once upon a time he led Britain's biggest boy band, was the sexiest, most charismatic star of his generation, and arguably the greatest white vocalist in pop history. Not only that, he was so moody and strange a whole mythology grew up around him. He walked away from fame when he could have become the new Sinatra. He was weirder than David Bowie, and too avant garde for Brian Eno. He's still alive today, but that's as much as anyone knows for sure. It's rumoured he likes to ride a bicycle to his local pub and play a game of darts. He's so mysterious that he makes Greta Garbo look like Denise Van Outen.
>
> All musicians like to think they're misfits, but Scott Walker really is. There was a deep divide in pop music in the 1960s, and Scott fell right down the middle of it. Where did he belong, exactly? Was it on TV, with all those squires of squaredom like Lovelace Watkins and Peter Gordeno? Should he wear a frilly shirt and a velvet bow tie and serenade the straights? Or was he a rock'n'roll renegade, whose music prowled the darkest reaches of the psyche and scared the crap out of people? Nobody was sure. You'd have to imagine Dean Martin singing Joy Division. And you'd still be baffled.

For a while though it all worked perfectly, and in 1965 Scott Walker was simply magnificent. Here's how Nik Cohn described him in his prime: "He was a light golden colour and he had all the equipment, the tragic mouth and misted eyes and fluttery lashes, the thin hands and soft hair, and he never managed more than a small sad smile. When he sang, his hands went up in front of his grieving face and, delicately, his body curled up like a lettuce leaf." This was brilliant pop theatre and a million women longed to mother him. You really have to wonder where it all went wrong. (**A profile of the fabulous Scott Walker, written for *GQ* magazine, July 2000.**)

Well it had little chance of going 'right' for long. It did go right for quite a while, but the music industry is a greedy monster. Scott was no one's idiot. Conflicts of interest pervaded his career. Neither was he 'strange'. To me he was what it was all about; other boys were strange. His voice was gold dust, but his original artistry took him in a different direction whenever it could. The time was wrong for Scott to enjoy full artistic freedom, but *fame* he could have grabbed by the bucket load. But fame didn't interest him too much. But like it or not he had it. He was the walking talking singing Golden Ticket to management and publicists alike. But he was *altogether too* valuable as a singer to those who made or broke careers. Voices like that are rare. Faces like that broke hearts. Talents like that made a lot of money, largely for other people.

But Scott is an Original Artist

But, it was like watching a real life drama of how to take a massively creative misfit and make him ' fit'. How he handled the pressure I had no idea at the time but yes there were hundreds like me who genuinely worried about him and his incredible talent. He didn't 'fit'. Would he ever 'fit'? (I will never forget the headline in one interview he gave: 'Money is a Monster that offends me Man'.) He could have so easily 'fitted' into a mega singing career. He chose not to and money was no incentive. Apparently no incentive at all. Not exactly a trait likely to endear him to some other 60's musical names who would have given their right arm for his voice alone. Like I said, stories like his are rare.

But as a young artist watching from afar, wow, this guy wasn't anything like any pop star I had seen before.

The BBC was impressed enough by him to give him a six week TV show. He had power of a sort, and respect, but then he had no real power at all. It was the 60's. Management came in two versions; Mr 10% and Mr 50% (Ok and a third version; Mr 99%). As far as management was concerned, imagination and original thinking was required with Scott. Best of luck with that then.

But Scott is the Magnificent Voice

For quite a while few people understood why his career went the way it did back then. Even today on a Facebook group I administrate, I see lamentations from those who would have preferred Scott stay 'the voice'. They can't understand why that wasn't enough for him. And I get that. I certainly had every reason to revere the voice. It would have been enough for 999 men out of a 1000 trying to make it big in music. It was a gift. That confused many people; good looks and a voice like that? What more does the guy need? Little wonder some started to consider him 'awkward'. He had enough 'gifts' to fill the lives of two artists; if not three. Does that make the role of an artist's manager easier? No of course not. In the 60's not a chance would be my guess. I eventually met a few managers and they were in a mould of their own.

'Do what I say and I will make you rich!' 'Do what I say and I will make you famous!'

Of course they were all way off cue; he wanted to develop as an artist and that was an alien concept in pop music in the 60's and probably wouldn't make them any money.

What every Young Artist needs is a Scott Engel in their life! Ordinary won't do!

But why didn't Scott want to settle for a massively respected singing career? He didn't just have the voice, he had enormous respect for the writers of great songs and in fact always credited them in his TV performances. Heaven knows he turned me on to so many great writers in music. To be opened up to those fabulous talents as young as I was, remains a very precious part of my education. He was cool enough to be totally uncool and get away with it, and quoted middle of the road singers Val Doonican and Mat Monroe as singers who sang well and knew about phrasing. I remember so many club cabaret acts quoting Scott and frankly imitating his song choices. I know some who still do.

He was still in his early 20s. Why wasn't he hungry for that kind of musical validity? An easy life in many respects; more BBC TV shows. Profitable recording contracts. Let's not even take his looks into the equation; no need. He could have been ugly with vocal chords like that. But of course he knew then, what we all know now, that audiences can be all too easily pleased.

So why? Where did that inexhaustible knowledge come from? Why wasn't an immediate fame fix ever going to be his aim? That alone separated him from the majority of his 1960's contemporaries. The bigger they were the more Scott bothered them, hence the notoriously repeated story that I remember first time round when Mick Jagger supposedly threw the contents of his ashtray at Scott in a nightclub. Jagger could, with the help of the Stones morph himself from an economics student from UCL to a pop star, but working out what Scott Engel was about was a puzzle they didn't hand out certificates for. They might have inhabited the same metaphorical stage but they were from different planets. Scott was a threat to many people. They just couldn't pin him down, or put him in a box. This guy came from Hollywood? No way. Mars more likely.

Oops the Rabbit is Out of the Hat!

Well it was bound to happen. There might not have been any internet back then, but a talent like that had a history and it made itself known. Scott had a past career.

Scott new what it was like to be a teenage 'artist'. Little wonder 'fame' was not an incentive; he had his teenage career behind him.

In the art of an artist re-inventing oneself, Scott did it for real not for effect. How many can say that?

In the UK with the Walker Brothers, it was his chance to start afresh, but he had already been a seasoned professional as a teenager. He was known nationally in the USA because of the TV shows he appeared on. He had recording contracts as a kid and during his teens. He was on the Broadway stage as a 10 year old child. The big deal however was the Eddie Fisher show (big prime time viewing syndicated nationwide USA), Scott was Fisher's 'protégé' (much the same as the Osmonds were to the Andy Williams show). He was on every week. He would have continued into a big 'Sinatra' style career, which was, understandably the plan, if Fisher hadn't discovered the joys of Elizabeth Taylor and left his wife Debbie Reynolds. The scandal at that time was a big deal, and so Scott had suddenly lost his 'mentor'.

Fate had clearly taken a hand in his artistic path too.

But I can certainly understand his reticence to talk about his teenage success as a teenybop star, which, given that I am currently writing this, I can totally get. There have been times, in fact many times, when I have glossed over my 'early' career. Not for any other reason other than it never cropped up. Who doesn't like to leave their adolescent years in the past when negotiating an adult career?

And Scott was 'cooool', really cool. Having his childhood career 'out there' was not what he needed when trying to conduct his career as a creative artist.

What his management thought when they found out was never publicised at the time. I even wonder if they ever knew all about 'Little Scotty Engel' when they signed him. I somehow doubt it. But Gary and John would have done.

Being a recognised talent when so young can be a strange place to be. It can be a time full of promise and full of hope, but difficult to negotiate nonetheless. Being singled out as a young talent is difficult for many. It separates you from others. It makes you different but it is also a chance to make a massive leap forward because of your youth. Or it did then. But more for boys than girls I remember thinking at the time.

So Scott was the creative blueprint I needed. Oh, not the blueprint of how to make money in music, or remain mindlessly famous, that's for sure. So maybe in today's celebrity culture he would have had an even worse time. But as a young idealist teenage creative in the making? He was manna from heaven. His artistry was even beginning to capture my complex father's interest.

Father Dear Father

One of the best things I gained from Scott though was a stronger relationship and understanding of my own complex and creative father. My father approved of the influence Scott had on me. In fact, he had a lot of admiration for him. He was a

Scott fan of a different generation, and when he heard Scott sing the Brel songs I was playing daily, he started to talk to me about his wartime experiences in Holland. ('Next' being one that really touched him) Scott built a very unlikely bridge between us. Why unlikely? Well it was a bridge based on his 14 year old daughter understanding of the reality of war. The value of a packet of nylons and a bar of soap to soldiers and women in a war zone, and the horror of his role during the war on Graves Commission in Holland. (When I was fifteen, an American guy came to our house asking for my father. He went to Dad's workplace to 'shake his hand'. It was Guy Gibson's brother. Dad never spoke about it but he picked up the remains of the great war hero Guy Gibson in Holland).

My father was also to give me a real insight into how the pop music business loved publicity. He proved to be a wizard at arranging for me to meet this star or that. Musician, sports stars, actors; all I had to do was a portrait, many of them for charity. But all for publicity. So at a very young age I met a lot of known names and also their management, publicity agents etc. Interesting bunch back in the 60's 70's. I learnt very young how to handle myself in such company. That prepared me in many ways to deal with myself as an artist. But this was unusual for an overweight kid from a Midland town; to have my own confidence on such a level. Very unusual given I was podgy little dolly girl for a while!

School — Mmmmmm

I was also off school a lot (painting and drawing and listening to music whilst I was 'ill') and I was 'known' in my town. I was followed by some younger girls in school and in as much as my father orchestrated my public 'career', he also allowed me to experience another side of life. I was allowed to go to coffee bars and I went to pubs with my leather jacketed friends. In my fourteenth year I would be in the pubs and clubs with my friends. I wore miniskirts and eye makeup like Dusty Springfield. I was to be found tearing around on the back of motor bikes (Dad didn't approve of that, … but hey) and of course the school got wind of some younger girls following me after school in to town. Yes, he was not an ordinary father. Like I said apparently, I didn't do ordinary, but then the 60's were not 'ordinary'.

The final straw was when our music teacher invited the class to take into the music class some of our current favourite pop music. I took in Scott's 'Next' and 'The Plague'. One was a Brel song of the brothel trucks, and 'queers' in the army and the other a Scott song, inspired by Camus, a truly monumental performance. My father loved both so as far as I was concerned a music teacher would at least see the merit in such music. No such luck. She was shocked. (Some of my school friends loved it). 'What a beautiful voice', my music teacher finally said. She didn't know what else to say.

My headmistress wanted me to toe the line and give a better example to the younger girls. My inappropriate choice of music hadn't helped. It wasn't enough for her that my name and her school were in the press weekly. So my father was invited to have a meeting with her whilst I stood outside her office waiting. I had told him what happened in the music lesson. I heard my father say to her eventually; 'Miss Hughes, I refuse to let my daughter's schooling interfere with her education'.

Go Dad!!!

Oh the Power of Coincidence

At the same time as my article in the Daily Mirror, the big news in the music industry and in the news generally was that Scott was reported to have been dragged from a gas filled flat. It was sensational news of course, and the source of much upset to many including me.

But I got over half a page in the Daily Mirror, and Scott's predicament was given tiny paragraph of coverage in that paper. Frankly I couldn't understand that at the time; my portraits could have been covered at any time. Scott in such a situation, be it intentional or not, was 'news'.

The Mirror photographer Bill Ellman and the journalist Bill Daniels (he ended up covering a few of my stories) on the night they took the pictures of me and the Mayor with the portraits in the Town Hall at Rugby, said something that my father and I couldn't understand. They referred to 'another' story: 'this is better than the other story—ha ha'; said in a manner which implied they were happy to have trumped some plan. They were clearly pleased as punch to have got my story even though they had to travel up from London and it was 10.30pm when the article was sent through to the Daily Mirror HQ.

But the 60's were notorious for publicity stunts, and on that front I doubt much has changed. The idea was, and still is, any publicity is good publicity. My story must have been like manna from heaven to Scott's management. That the gas filled flat incident actually happened has not been disputed (Scott made no real statement at the time and some time later in an interview referred to it as a stupid mistake fuelled by drink and medication.) That a 60's publicist would have milked it for all it was worth was a strong possibility.

The following morning I went to my mother's place of work (they had a telephone—we never had one at home) and I rang Brian Somerville's office (Scott's publicist; I had his number by then) and asked how Scott was, in the light of the recent news. (At the time I thought nothing of it but later in my life I realised that this was a bold thing to do) I wondered if he would speak to me. My mother retold this story often, given that she watched it at the time so it was pretty much embedded in my memory;

'My name is Heather Johnston and my portraits of The Walker Brothers were in the Daily Mirror.' He came to the phone, I said 'I want to know how Scott is?' 'Scott is fine Heather. This story was (he actually said this to me) *blown up out of all proportion.*' (All publicists mantra then and probably now). My response; 'Well not in the Daily Mirror it wasn't Mr Sommerville'. He then said; 'Fantastic story Heather and wonderful portraits.'

I wrote it down in the shop where Mum worked. Scott was fine. All was well and I got off the phone still suspicious; always the best way with publicists. I'm not sure what I really believed when it came down to the health and welfare of Scott. Yes, I was still only fourteen and I remember my mother looking on with her mouth wide open, 'Who were you just speaking to?' Scott's publicity manager, I said. 'He loved the portraits and said it made a fantastic story, and Scott is fine'.

Meeting with the group

The Walker Brothers toured a lot. I went to all the tours. By the time of the 66 tour with the Troggs, ad Dave Dee and Co, the press 'arranged' it for me to go backstage. At that time I had only met Gary of course. Scott around that time had had his famous 'short haircut'.

Coventry Theatre 1966 the Walker Brothers Tour and talk in the press about Irene Dunford refusing Scott's Marriage proposal. I was backstage and met up with John and Gary. It was good meeting Gary again. I had completed a portrait of John and his two puppies Scotch and Brandy; the cover shot of Rave magazine a month or two earlier. I had broken my finger in my right hand playing Tennis at school and completed much the portrait in difficulty with my right hand, so used my left hand. (I met John again some years after. He told me he kept that portrait for some time, but he thought it had gone with one of his wives!) The press took photos backstage of me handing over the portrait to John.

Scott was around; we knew it by a flurry of interest by everyone and then he was gone. The Scarlet Pimpernel. I saw him, in his blue reefer blazer covered (literally) with professional SLR cameras hung around his shoulders. It seems that was his escape route from face to face confrontation that month. He was dashing about like a photographer on a mission, onto the roof terrace of the Coventry Theatre. Certainly no interrupting allowed. It was respected. I respected it. The mood backstage was amazing. I had been backstage for a few things before by then, but knowing Scott was around was electric. The other bands as popular as they were just didn't pack that charisma, and there was the distinct feeling that they were collectively in awe of Scott. Great bands of the 60's they were. But the buzz backstage was only about one person.

This was the first time I really witnessed the massive respect and admiration for Scott amongst the other acts. I also witnessed a degree of 'Scott who?' off a couple of guys backstage. He was too much competition for many I'm sure, and there was always a chance of resentment. Was he aloof? I think his 'legend' went before him. Was he intimidating? I didn't think so but his reputation was. His reputation was Marilyn Monroe and James Dean proportions, both of whom would have had trouble competing in the raw 'talent' stakes with Scott Engel. One thing was for sure, he was under some pressure.

I was there but I was lucky. Backstage wasn't exactly teeming with fans, but I was someone who got page three coverage in the Daily Mirror and, evidently, that was currency.

I wasn't the kind of fan who went weak at the knees. The only times I came unstuck was when the roadies took me back to the front stalls to get my seat and I was noticed. I learnt very quickly to avoid those situations. To be taken from backstage to theatre through the side door was to tell the fans you had been backstage. Never again. Girls from my school were in the front row and I got pulled to the ground. The roadies did a great job of getting me out. My parents were always with me but not in the actual concert theatre. They only ever saw one Walker Brothers show at the North Pier in Blackpool, and later John's new Walker Brothers, but whilst I was watching the show they would be outside watching the crowds and dreading hearing ambulances; another commonplace happening at Walker Brothers concerts.

So at that point I had met Gary twice and John once. Only one to go. But it would be 2 years before that happened.

Meanwhile I was still doing portraits and as many different kinds of faces as possible. I was particularly keen on portraits in dramatic lighting conditions. A preference that was to prove to be a key to my eventual creative direction.

President Kennedy

I enjoyed exploring different faces with my portraiture. I completed portraits of Dusty Springfield, Francoise Hardy, and Mohamed Ali, for an exhibition in Rugby (my first), but the most notable portrait was one I completed of the late John F Kennedy.

I was just eleven years old when he was assassinated and like most people, I was destined to remember that event since. It was the first ever 'Newsflash' I have ever seen on TV and I think it was in the middle of Coronation Street. I was shocked by it to say the least, and I remember watching all the follow up reports; The Warren Commission I watched for hours on end. I went to the local library and found—the wonderful photo by Canadian photographer Karsch, in a book about the late President Kennedy. I liked that picture from an artistic perspective that I didn't know back then I even possessed. My fascination with the Kennedy situation was enough inspiration to complete the piece. At that age I was not politically inclined, but I was moved by his death, and it seemed so was so many people worldwide.

My father decided what to do with it; send it to the White House'. On Friday 12th May 1967, the portrait was sent air freight to Washington. The press covered the story, the air freight company covered the costs, and I ended up two months later contracted to the BBC, and appeared on Midlands News, and then the National news. (I was paid 3 guineas by the BBC. They still dealt in guineas!) The portrait went to the White House and I received a letter from Lyndon B Johnson saying, thank you very much and that it was to be sent to the National Archives gallery in Washington. The press thought it would be a good idea for me I go to the US, but my father thought differently and he would not let me go on my own. (As I was later to learn, I would find it difficult to leave home at all.) I found myself on a TV programme being asked questions about US politics.

Poet Rupert Brooke

My next subject was Rugby born poet Rupert Brooke. I grew up in a house literally round the corner from his family home. The portrait of him eventually found a home in the library of the Kings College Cambridge, and I was befriended by a lovely

Cambridge Don, Mr John Saltmarsh, who invited me and my parents to dine with him in his rooms above the Kings College chapel. I loved Cambridge university. I loved the smell of it and the feel of it. John Saltmarsh sent me cards for many years at Christmas.

Other portraits followed and all were the subject of much local and or national publicity. (More in the biography section of www.heatherharmanartist.com)

The real learning however was when I experimented with head angles profiles, and high contrast lighting conditions to light the face. Luckily most of the time that involved Scott's face. One of the most photographed faces of the 60's. I did most of my learning and developing into portraiture using Scott's face. I almost could get a likeness of Scott with my eyes shut. I probably still could and I haven't portrayed him in years. But I was aware of the need to learn.

So it was the work I was doing for my own satisfaction that I enjoyed the most. The work that I felt I had learned something from, rather than the work which got a lot of publicity. An early lesson to learn.

Manager Dad

But around about this time I was also experiencing a difficulty with my father. My father was one of those inventive wordsmiths who could think up an advertising slogan in a second; quick of mind and witty. I was growing up of course, but my father was trying to influence my subject choices too much and it became an issue. He was clearly enjoying his role as artist's father and 'manager'. But the more he 'managed' the more he got results, and some of the perks were undoubtedly enjoyable. But, I was in an increasingly uncomfortable position. I loved and respected him and we had an incredibly frank relationship (his name was also Frank) but it was becoming more and more difficult.

Back in Edinburgh as the youngest son in a large Catholic family, he was known as Franky the poet. He loved words, but the war took care of any ambitions he might have had to pursue his love of writing.

My friends were intrigued by my parents. My father being more intellectual and poetic and my mother who was in so many ways the polar opposite. She was incredible and funny and loved my father with a passion but had no real idea where his head was. So I grew up more or less a conduit between them. I 'got' Dad, in a way that Mum didn't. So from an early age I remember her saying to me, ' You go and tell your Dad this or that. You know him better than I do!'

So my friends concluded he was like Einstein and Mum was like Lucille Ball. About right, but they had a marvelous and happy marriage.

But my father was complex, and frankly had it not been for Scott's choice of music in the 60's, highly unusual choices like Jacques Brel, which Dad related to from his own war time experiences, I'm not sure we would have as great an understanding as father and daughter. Scott's music gave Dad an opportunity to talk to me, and he took that opportunity. Could it have been anyone else's music ? Not a chance. The major musical commentators of the time were nowhere near Brel or Scott's own work. Dylan would not have done Brel.

Growing up

Yes he did allow me a separate life; only very few people knew that Heather Johnston the artist was the same Heather that they knew in my leather jacket down the coffee bar. But my real friends did. When the eye make went on—and the kinky boots (thigh high) I was just Heather. This is also what my school did not approve of, of course. It was the days of Mods and Rockers, and I was a Rocker. If the press had found out ... ooops. I think Dad took a wicked delight at seeing me negotiate what became a double life.

One lunchtime I got a lift back to school on the back of a friend's bike. It wasn't the first time and my biker friends all knew I had to be dropped off round the corner from school. He thought he would have a joke and took me through the school grounds on the back of his Norton Black Prince and dropped me off outside the headmistress's office window! Oh dear. Me and my Gondola basket disappeared pretty quickly!

The following day was a Saturday and I was in London at a formal dinner with the Duke and Duchess of Beaufort, Cilla Black and Anthony Newley. The week after I was in London again, I was completing a portrait for the Spina Bifida charity of Harry Secombe. (My cousin Michelle was born in 1966, with

Spina Bifida and our family was devastated by her diagnosis at the time.) The charity was run by Tom Ravensdale, an ornithologist, married to Saroya, a belly dancer who met us at the train station in Tom's Rolls Royce. Tom hit the headlines for having a custom motor bike; it had a stereo and a tea maker in the fairing. You couldn't make this up! Only in the 60's? What a time. We were taken back to Euston station later that day in the Roller.

I was in the papers or TV on a regular basis. I was 'The Rugby Artist', and Dad did really love his role of Father and Manager.

But school was still an issue. It was a good school for girls. My artistic reputation was something they were proud of (because the school got a regular mention in the press). At school, I was a model schoolgirl. I always was. So much illness up to the age of fourteen did mean that I was usually on catch up in some subjects but my grades were good. I might have been off school a lot but I kept my grades up. In some ways I think that annoyed the school. So I had a couple of snide comments made to me, one from my art teacher who could never claim that anything I did was the result of her teaching, but I can't remember such comments from my school friends. 'Why is it every time you are off school you end up with something in the papers?' kind of comments.

The school also contacted my parents and were annoyed that they should have excused me from school so as to attend funerals. 'It is impossible to believe that Heather should be attending so many funerals in such a short time Mr Johnston'. In fact it was entirely possible. I attended 9 funerals within a period of about 18 months within the Rocker/biker community. Of course that fact did nothing to make the school feel any better.

He was an unusual Dad, but as time went on the situation between us was not going to be comfortable. Looking back Dad gave me a degree of personal freedom, but artistic freedom was not so easy for him to give me.

At the same time, I was watching Scott's career and work develop and he took control in whatever way he could of his own artistic path. Still, his management and everyone else in the music industry, would talk of the second Sinatra.

What they never reckoned on was the 'first Scott Engel'. And yet I have had sympathy for Scott's management. Oh boy what a joke. To be handed Scott Engel, his looks, his charm, his incomparable voice, and the way he commanded respect from so many people in the music industry. How at his young age he had so much experience; but was not one jot bothered about material wealth. That would not have made him a straight forward act to 'manage' and even less easy to sway with the promise of riches.

Art College?

I wanted to get into more of my art. Dad wanted me to get more into publicity and promotion because he was good at it. In fact he enjoyed it. I wanted to go to art school, to be honest I knew Dad did not want that. He wanted me at home as did Mum. Art school was 'somewhere away from home'. I don't think that they had given my further education in art a thought. It just wasn't on our family's radar. At one point I was invited around an art school (the nearest to home) just me and my parents and the teachers. I was fascinated (I was fifteen then) but Dad looked at the work produced, beautiful drawings of cabbages and cross sections of mushrooms and made his mind up there and then. He knew that wouldn't be the art I wanted to do so he then knew that I 'needed' him.

I must be honest and say I wasn't massively impressed at the kind of work on show either. As good as it was I wanted to learn way more than that. I was into portraiture and the human form and the 60's that was London based. It was the time of the commercial artist. Courses were basically 'commercial art' biased. The teachers suggested I would be a candidate for The Royal Academy in London (away from home) and also a place I had never heard of back then called Slade (also in London and 'away from home'.) One of them went as far as contact my art teacher at school to make sure some people were on the same page. Good luck with that I thought. The truth is of course, college was not on the radar for me. I was a girl, and girls in my family had for decades followed the same path; maybe a job, then marriage. No one in my family had ever gone to university; male or female.

Meeting Scott

By early 1968 I was just sixteen and developing into colour in my portraits. It is amazing I had waited so long with colour being a major inspiration to me, but I was happy in black and white for a long time. Artistically that was a great thing. I often tell my students today that putting colour to one side every now and again is a great learning curve. By that time I had made a few friends in the local and National press and TV. So when Scott went solo from the band and embarked on his first solo tour, it was arranged that I meet him.

Yeah right I thought. Arranging it was the simple bit. Pulling it off would be another matter altogether. By that time Scott's reputation was through the roof. He could do no wrong. He even had the great jazz musician Ronnie Scott and his musicians accompany him around the country; like they were his own personal band; that was the level of respect Scott then had after the release of his first and second solo albums. Then there was his TV show. Six weeks for the BBC. He was just 24.

One problem was that as soon as the tour was announced my school friends knew I would be going to meet him. They just knew. And they guessed it would be either Coventry or Leicester or Birmingham. They didn't even ask me. Their plan was to attempt to stick to me like glue.

The meeting was going to be Coventry on his last night of his tour. By that time word was out in the music press;

> *Scott was meeting no one on his tour.*

I told my school friends this and they believed me because they had read it too and because well, frankly, it would have been easier to meet the Beatles. No one met Scott as easily as that, it seemed. The other acts on his tour (The Casuals, Gun, Paper Dolls, Cupids Inspiration) had all reported back to the music press that they had not even met Scott and there was only one week of the tour to go! This was not looking good. I would have said my chances were slim to none.

So I had no real idea what was going to happen when I got to the Coventry Theatre—quite early on the Sunday, of October 1968.

I suppose that up until that point, when my father and the press arranged something for me it was a given; it would happen. But with the Scott meeting I said very little at home. Neither did Dad. On the other hand I had been some two or three years hearing 'this' about Scott and 'that' about Scott. That he wasn't meeting everyone on his tour was no surprise. He really called his own shots as much as he could, much of the time on such things. Frankly as long as he was working and creating I was happy. If he wanted to meet me he would and if he didn't he wouldn't. Pragmatic me.

But on the day I had my portrait prepared. An important one to me; it was my first all colour portrait and I had worked a long time on it and was happy enough with it. I was giving it to Scott. Maybe. I borrowed my cousin's new black crochet dress; put on my Dusty Springfield makeup, did my hair, popped on my leather coat, black boots (a typical Dolly Bird as they were called then) and went to Coventry, taking along a good friend in the car along with my father, and my cousin driving. My friend at the Daily Sketch, Dave Adams, had arranged the meeting, but wasn't going to attend it. (I was surprised at that but later found out that Dave agreed the terms of the meeting with Scott's manager, Maurice King, with Scotts permission. One proviso was that there would be no publicity). I remember being happy about that, (apart from the fact that the press always sent me photos of meetings with my subjects.

We arrived early, sometime in the early afternoon). I took my Kodak Instamatic and a few flash cubes.

I knew my way round the backstage area of the Coventry Theatre, so we headed through all the right doors and asked one of the security guys for Maurice King (Scott's manager) and was taken to the green room. We were introduced to Mary Arnold, Maurice Kings wife, and we all sat at the bar. Now the green room at the Coventry theatre isn't massive, but it was certainly full. All the bands on the tour were in the bar, sitting around tables, just generally doing what they did on tours, hanging out until it was time to go on stage. I became a point of interest. I wasn't on the tour so who was I? One of the braver guys in the Gunn, came straight up and asked me, so Mary introduced me and said I was there to meet Scott. (Oh dear, was I really?) The look on his face was precious and the room became quiet.

That was the start of an interesting afternoon.

Now it is one thing reading in the press that no one on the tour had met Scott and another thing to see their reaction when they heard the news that I was to do just that. They didn't believe it, and they started to make fun of the situation; and of me. 'She thinks she is going to meet 'HIM'. 'HA HA'. You get the idea. Much derision and fun was had at my expense that afternoon. All pretty polite but uncomfortable all the same. Mary Arnold just said 'ignore them'. It was a long afternoon to be ignoring them. One by one they all finally went on stage and did their bit and then back to the green room and more beer and sandwiches.

As far as I could make out there were none of Ronnie Scott's band around; and Mary Arnold confirmed that. At one point Tiger Mathis of the Paper Dolls came in and headed straight for us. (The Paper Dolls were more or less 'proteges' of Mary Arnold). She also wanted to know who I was and where did I get my black crochet dress (girls talk eh!) ? She and the band had got silver versions of the same dress to go on stage. When she heard I was to meet Scott she told me straight out 'No Kidding—no way!'. Tiger Mathis was a great personality and a lot of fun. She helped the afternoon along with her stories and laughs. But the rest of the bands were relentless all afternoon. Quite funny really. What amazed me at the time is that Mary Arnold said nothing. She just ignored them. Now that did seem odd, unless she was just so used to that behaviour.

What I don't remember about that day were timings. At some point Maurice King came for me. How did I feel? I am often asked that. Well by that time I remember feeling indignant. Why? To start with as I walked down the stairs to the dressing rooms with Maurice King, a handful of jokers from the bands followed us, pretending they were creeping silently, down the stairs to the backstage area, cameras in hand; and stayed looking around the stairwell where they could see everything. More jibes—'It won't happen' She won't get to meet him? (I heard later they took bets).

The truth is they did me a favour. Whilst I was niggled by them

I had little time to think. I found myself outside Scott's dressing room.

As I write this I am thinking of Midge Ure's quote:

'It is not very often you get to meet your heroes. And it is not very often if you do meet them that you are actually quite pleased you did meet them'.

There were many times before that day that I had chance to actually think about the fact I was due to meet Scott. So I had time to get used to the idea and if it didn't happen so be it. But by then I was 3 months off my seventeenth birthday and I had achieved quite a lot since the Walker Brothers portraits in the Town Hall. I was also very aware that I was going into a room to meet my idol, my muse and my mentor in many ways. My respect had no boundaries and it was in fact a massive risk, in case this guy was a real disappointment. I would have been destroyed. Not to mention devastated. Only twelve months before Scott was given the chance to meet Jacques Brel, and he declined because he was scared to meet someone who might not meet his expectations. I get that.

The first thing I remember is hearing Scott's voice—calling for Ronnie (Scott). Sounds of a saxophone in the next dressing room. I walked in head high and Scott walked up smiling and grabbed my hand and shook it. Introductions were made all round. His big smile did little to help my state of mind but he took over.

I was looking at Scott, wearing his stage makeup, which made his eyes seem even bluer. He was looking at my portrait and he was clearly impressed. 'What did you use?' 'Pastel Scott' 'How does that work?' he asked, 'Well it is in stick form". The conversation went on. I told him all about the medium and how to use it and that it was my first portrait using colour, which he found hard to believe. So we chatted about my first portraits and the Town Hall business, but mainly about pastel and the new portrait; about art, and that he was a keen artist. He talked about his love of charcoal sketching. He mentioned his art college experience in California.

I had a photo taken — with my little Kodak Instamatic. Back then it wasn't common to rattle off dozens of photos unless you were the press or Dezo Hoffman.

Then he said — 'Art college' When are you going to art college? My father was busy with Maurice King so I told him quietly that 'it is difficult'. I knew by then that my parents were not happy about me leaving home at all. I said ' Where I live there are no colleges for art. He nodded, but then he did something amazing and looking directly at my father said, ' I just told Heather that she must go to a real good Art College Mr Johnston.' He smiled that charming smile. He took my Dad by surprise and he just nodded.

Oh yes this guy was my hero! Up to my expectations? And some! It was like meeting someone I had 'known' for some time. For the first time all day I actually felt relaxed. Midge Ure? How weird is that? I felt comfortable and actually meeting someone who could talk art, and he was genuinely interested in how the medium worked; this was something I wasn't used to. I never 'talked' art to anyone. Strange but true. I don't think

I had met anyone who had been to art college either.

I asked Scott if he was going to keep the portrait? He said yes and that he had just got a new flat with his girlfriend, and it would go on one of the walls. (OK, that I found hard to believe. Scott putting an image of himself on his flat wall? Nah). But that is the measure of the man. Maurice was keen to get us all out and get Scott on stage. Scott seemed in no hurry. I was quite willing to go and find my seat, but he was still talking, so he took my elbow and I was walking to the stage with him.

'You make sure you get to art college Heather. You have real talent and must get good training.' 'My parents aren't keen for me to leave home Scott'. He sighed and nodded. Those blue eyes seared through me.

And as we reached the wings he grabbed hold of both my hands inside both of his—looked at me and said, 'work to do'. He smiled at me. Was he nervous? Hard to say. He didn't seem so and he strode out onto that stage like he owned it. It was the last night of his tour and he seemed happy and confident and above all professional. By that time Ronnie Scott was stood by me waiting for his cue.

It was a great privilege for me to meet Ronnie Scott too. When I was 10 years old I started taking saxophone lessons from an old friend of Ronnie; Ted Morris—who played in the Val Parnell orchestra at the London Palladium for years. Ted died just after my second lesson.

I never did get to my seat. I watched the show from the wings. (But I had seats to the second show too so I saw the show twice). I went to collect my friend, and took her up to the Green room. Dad was there. With my head held high I smiled. Mary Arnold was still there too. We chatted and for once the guys in the bands were 'quiet'.

It was reported in the music press the following week that with it being the tours last night at Coventry, he invited all band members back to his room after the shows were over. They all reported what a lovely man he was. What more could they say? He was. I found speaking to him easier than speaking to many.

Later I drew a comparison between the backstage experience with Scott and that of two years before, both at the Coventry theatre. In 1966, it was pretty frantic and chaotic backstage, Dave Dee, Dozy, Beaky Mick And Tich, The Troggs; a lot of people gagging around. As I have already written Scott was dodging all the chaos; disappearing on the roof with his cameras. Whenever on the move he seemed to be on urgent business; if he walked back into the backstage area three or four people wanted him, Scott this and Scott that; all wanting something. He could have had no peace.

In 1968, his friend Ronnie Scott toured with him and that was an honour in itself, but Scott commanded that kind of respect. But Ronnie and his band the finest musicians, gave Scott the space and the atmosphere of calm; a few Jazz notes from one dressing room and a few from another. Different atmosphere altogether. Hence no one visiting backstage, not even the other groups and acts on the tour. Mary told me later that the reason the green room was jam pack full was because there was no room backstage in the dressing room areas, Scott and Ronnie and his band had that area, and it seemed to me that between them they called the shots and Scott had his peace and a better touring experience probably for the first time since arriving in the UK.

'I just told Heather that she must go to a real good Art College Mr Johnston.'

I knew that unless I managed to find a college where I was excited about the work I would not have the emotional strength to convince my parents to let me go. Meanwhile neither of them were looking for colleges for me of course. But what I needed was a plan, and to know that what I was so good at, I could build on and improve.

The situation with my father and his 'managing' me was still a real problem. I knew that great careers were not made by publicity alone. Scott had taught me that, but Dad wanted to prove differently. It was bound to cause problems sooner or later.

I felt trapped. I could see no way out of it. You can sack a manager but not a father. At one point he told me outright that he was the artist and he was just 'using my hands'. I couldn't pick up a pencil without him looking over my shoulder. He wanted me to draw who he chose, not who I chose which is a real recipe for disaster for any artist. At that point I could see no way forward. It was becoming oppressive, and because I could see no way out, I withdrew; literally. I dropped out of school just before my A levels. What was the point in them if there was going to be trouble with me going to art school or university? I was an only child and having siblings may have helped, and being a boy would also have been an advantage back then. Meanwhile I got a job in a television rental company for a while; I needed the breathing space, and my cousin was working there. Of course Scott's words about art college were ringing in my head.

After a few weeks I looked up from my desk to see my art teacher from school. She had come to talk some sense into me; I needed to go to art college! She was upset that I was where I was. There was little I could say to her, certainly not that I needed to get my father off my back, and I could see no artistic future.

'Didn't Time Sound Sweet Yesterday?'

That Scott's career was 'unconventional' is an understatement. How he got away with his song choices on his various TV appearances is testament to the respect he commanded in the entertainment industry as well as the music world. But it was often uncomfortable. I took to banning everyone from the room when Scott was on TV. I 'taped' everything he did, and still have those original tapes. But some of those performances were wonderful in the fact they were so bizarre. Hearing him sing Brel's 'My Death', on a prime time light entertainment show, (Billy Cotton Band Show rings a bell) and 'Boy Child' on another, (Nana Mouskouri Show) was surreal. He still didn't 'fit', but he did what he had to do.

Around about this time Scott's career was also heading in a negative direction. Scott 4 had been released, and contractual troubles began. Who would have guessed? Scott 4 is arguably one of his finest albums but without the backing of the record company, much could and did go wrong. It was painful to see the album fail to chart as high as the previous three albums had done. Clearly Scott had a lot invested his creativity in this album (his name reverting to Engel as opposed to 'Walker' was a way of making a stand for his artistic freedom). It was all his own compositions and a truly fabulous album; and considered a masterpiece even now.

But I had my own problems.

I loved my parents and did not realise what 'let me down' meant. I only knew that my options were severely limited. I realised that I had somehow missed the boat; a massive opportunity to develop my creativity. The one thing my father could not make me do was draw or paint. That was out of his control.

My family decided to make a move and follow their dream and move from Rugby. I was hoping the move would be south, to the London area. But their dream was to move to Blackpool. I had no say in it. That year I became engaged to my boyfriend Will, who had known me since I was 14 years old. Will was and remains my rock. He has been through everything with me. Yes he was one of my biker friends a very clever man as a mechanic and engineer and craftsman in his own right. And 100% different from my father as chalk is to cheese.

So to Blackpool we went, and Will and I were married within 6 months of our move. I was surrounded by domesticity and settling in to a new town. The wedding took up a lot of my creativity; I designed and made all of my families wedding outfits and my wedding dress with the help of master pattern cutter Will. A year later I gave birth to our daughter Deborah; living in a town not known for its value to a budding portrait artist. I was now a Mum.

The Power Struggle

Like most new young mums, my world was about my daughter, and that was fine by me. She was the centre of my world as it should be. The power struggle between myself and my father was largely unspoken, but that is what it was. That it shouldn't have been happening, and he shouldn't have put me in the position I found myself in, is true. But at the time I don't think it occurred to me that he was being selfish. Others might have disagreed, but I thought he was trying to do what he thought was the best for me, or I wanted to believe that.

One way or another, I know that I would never have put my daughter in that position.

When Debs was two years old, I enrolled in a History of Art course at the local college and also an Art A level course, just so that I could say that I had completed my Art A level, and to get me out of the house doing something I loved. My father got belligerent about my 'not following my art career' but what he meant was his idea of what my career should be. A career based on publicity. He would often bring up the fact that I had 'given up' my art, and I was stupid to do so. I hadn't given up anything, I had gotten myself from under his control. Dad would come up with controversial ideas for portraits that he knew or thought the press would love. I didn't.

What I didn't realise at the time was that my new status as a mother had a real effect on the power struggle between us. He adored his new granddaughter, as did Mum, and my grandparents. Debs became the centre of the household as babies do, but it is the mums who rule; when she could and could not be picked up taken out in the pram etc. Suddenly I wasn't just 'daughter' I was a mother in my own right, and with that 'promotion' came a new respect from my father.

So I continued my college evenings two a week which both got me into my work again and gave me a little 'me' time too.

Where was Scott?

I still read the Music press. Keeping track of what Scott was doing was getting difficult. But so much had changed. I took my daughter into town to pick up my latest albums, 'Till the Band comes In', 'Any Day Now', The 'Moviegoer'; each one (for me) testament to the strange position he had found himself in. New management; bad decisions or possibly no decisions at all; new family himself, responsibilities etc. But the music was a reflection of a man without a muse. His mojo gone. His passion seemed diminished. He seemed to be going through the motions on most of the tracks, with a few notable exceptions. It wasn't Scott as far as I was concerned; it was like he had 'switched himself off'. I was pretty unhappy it all. Scott shouldn't have been in this position. All was not well in my world.

It never occurred to me at the time but in fact I was going through something much the same as he was at the time. Struggling to be my own artist. It was some years alter I realised this. He was still on the TV but not doing what he wanted to do; not his own original work, and sometimes it was painful to watch. Anyone who knew his music knew that. It seemed he was doing what was necessary to get by; and I hated that.

Meeting John Maus again

Debs would have been 6 months old. I picked up the Blackpool Evening Gazette and there was an advert:

'Live at the Victoria Hotel, Cleveleys—The New Walker Brothers'. 'WHAT!

I didn't want to go. If you were to ask me why I probably couldn't have told you. Mum was excited and wanted to go. Dad ditto.

We all went along, and John was more than happy to have someone to spend time with from the 'old Walker Brothers' days. He was touring around with some of the NDO (Northern Dance Orchestra) and a guy from the Blackpool area called Jimmy singing Scott's parts, and that was the new Walker Brothers. (Jimmy had sung with them some years before I was told).

The show was excellent, well rehearsed and polished, as John would have it, and my Father being my Father, had taken my cuttings book to Cleveleys and John was very happy to spend a few hours sharing memories and having a few drinks. He was talking about the Rolling Stones a lot have spent some time in the south of France with them (Honky Chateau), and he was clearly besotted by Bianca Jagger.

The conversation turned to Scott of course. It was bound to. I asked about him. He had seen him the year before. He was OK. Gary was OK but had been very ill, according to John. One of the old roadies turned up backstage, Arthur Howarth. He said he remembered me from the Daily Mirror story. It seems Arthur was a boxer when younger and became a valued member of the road staff for the group. He had seen Scott the month previously backstage at some theatre with Mette and the baby. (Scott's daughter Lee had been born 4 months after I had Deborah). Scott was fine he said.

So a good evening was had by all, John spoiling my mother yet again, which she loved. John could be very charming and it was a great evening which he clearly enjoyed too.

But backstage with John, I realised I had moved on from the Walker Brothers, more than I thought. So I went along, but I don't think I even took a camera. I was one who wanted Scott to leave the band and go solo. But John was enjoying being back on the road with Jimmy who did great job 'being Scott' it must be said.

Out of the Creative Closet

A couple of years on, I had passed my A level art and History of Art and had started to work (art) again. Quietly, in my own room, during the day. I would draw Debs most of the time, or her friends. Or work from old master's drawings. The idea was to work without my father getting involved, which meant all traces of what I was doing needed to be packed away prior to him coming home from work; I just didn't want the hassle. (We all lived together back then) Eventually I got a bit lax about this and forgot the time when he arrived back to the house. Within a few days he said to me that he knew that I was 'doing my art' again, and that;

'I don't mind giving you my opinion if you will accept my criticisms'.

Clearly he saw me as coming to my senses and willing to return to his management.

I responded by going and grabbing my growing pile of art books from the library—(Gombrich—History of Art' being just one), and dropping them at his feet and said;

'OK you can start by reading those, and in a couple of years' time when you have gone through the list of other books you need to read, I will listen to your opinion'.

The look of astonishment on Dads face was the moment I knew that that was the moment I reclaimed my artistic freedom. I had gained my self respect. He didn't get upset. But he was left speechless. I had made my point and I think he respected that. From then on I didn't hide my work from him at the end of the day. I just didn't invite him to see it or involve him. I couldn't risk his ruining what was becoming a better relationship between us, and a new learning and growth process in my work.

I wonder if he ever really understood the creative 'handcuffs' he had me wrapped in as a teenager. How he had allowed his own creative ego to take me over?

So I turned the tables on him. I told him it was about time he got on with his own work, his writing. I pushed him to concentrate on his own work and in turn he left mine alone.

Difficult times. I am writing about them now, with difficulty.

*The Opening of Bletchley Disci record store -
Bletchely Chronicle and Echo 1966*

*The Opening of Bletchley Disci record store -
Bletchely Chronicle and Echo 1966*

*The Opening of Bletchley Disci record store -
Bletchely Chronicle and Echo 1966*

*Daily Mirror - Bill Ellman photographer - with the Mayor -
Stanley Carter. Aug 15th 1966*

HEATHER'S POP SKETCH LANDS THE MAYOR IN A RUMPUS

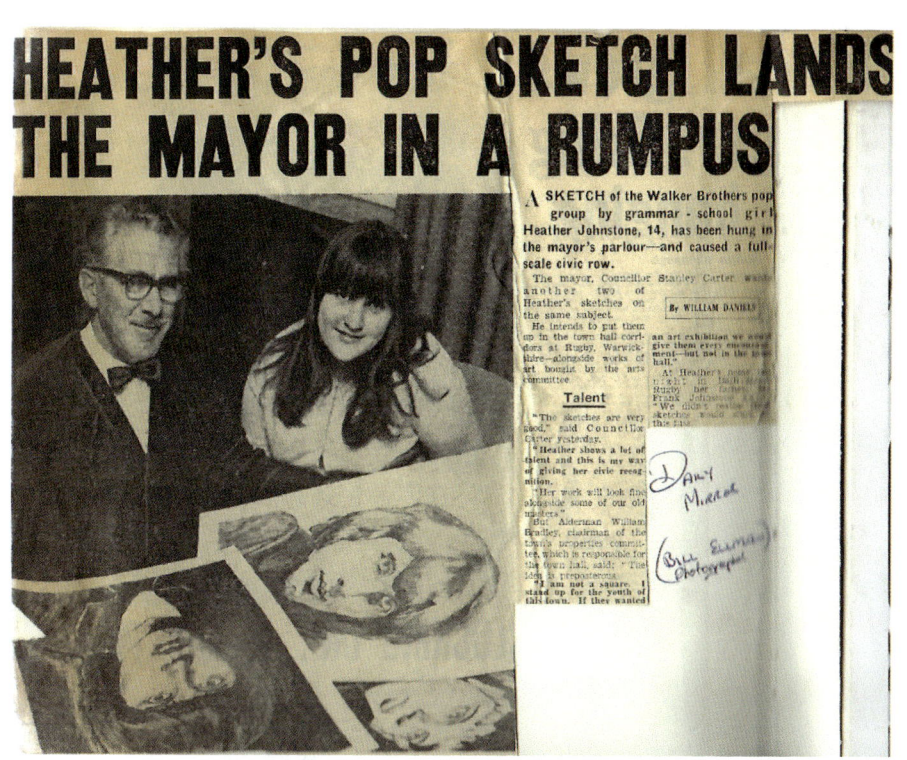

By WILLIAM DANIELS

A SKETCH of the Walker Brothers pop group by grammar-school girl Heather Johnstone, 14, has been hung in the mayor's parlour—and caused a full-scale civic row.

The mayor, Councillor Stanley Carter, wants another two of Heather's sketches on the same subject.

He intends to put them up in the town hall corridors at Rugby, Warwickshire—alongside works of art bought by the arts committee.

Talent

"The sketches are very good," said Councillor Carter yesterday.

"Heather shows a lot of talent and this is my way of giving her civic recognition.

"Her work will look fine alongside some of our old masters."

But Alderman William Bradley, chairman of the town's properties committee, which is responsible for the town hall, said: "The idea is preposterous.

"I am not a square. I stand up for the youth of this town. If they wanted an art exhibition we would give them every encouragement—but not in the town hall."

At Heather's home last night in Bath-street, Rugby, her father, Frank Johnston, said: "We didn't realise the sketches would cause this fuss."

Daily Mirror article - published page 3, 16th August 1966

Dear Pet Heather

Chiswick W4
Ron Kiss
16/8/64

This publisty will put you on top. Your Drawing Are most Exlent I seen This will give you The chance The Artist wants, They are very like like wish you All The Luck

Best wishes

Look on

R Kiss

Scott's postcard

*With John and Gary backstage - Coventry theatre
(Dave Dee Troggs Walker Brothers Tour 1966)*

*Scott and Heather in his dressing room
Coventry Theatre 25th October 1968*

*Heather with Maisie Van Courtland, London
for Ralph Gurnett meeting 1986*

*Following:
Four sketches completed from
Maisie's Walker Brothers Newsletter 1983*

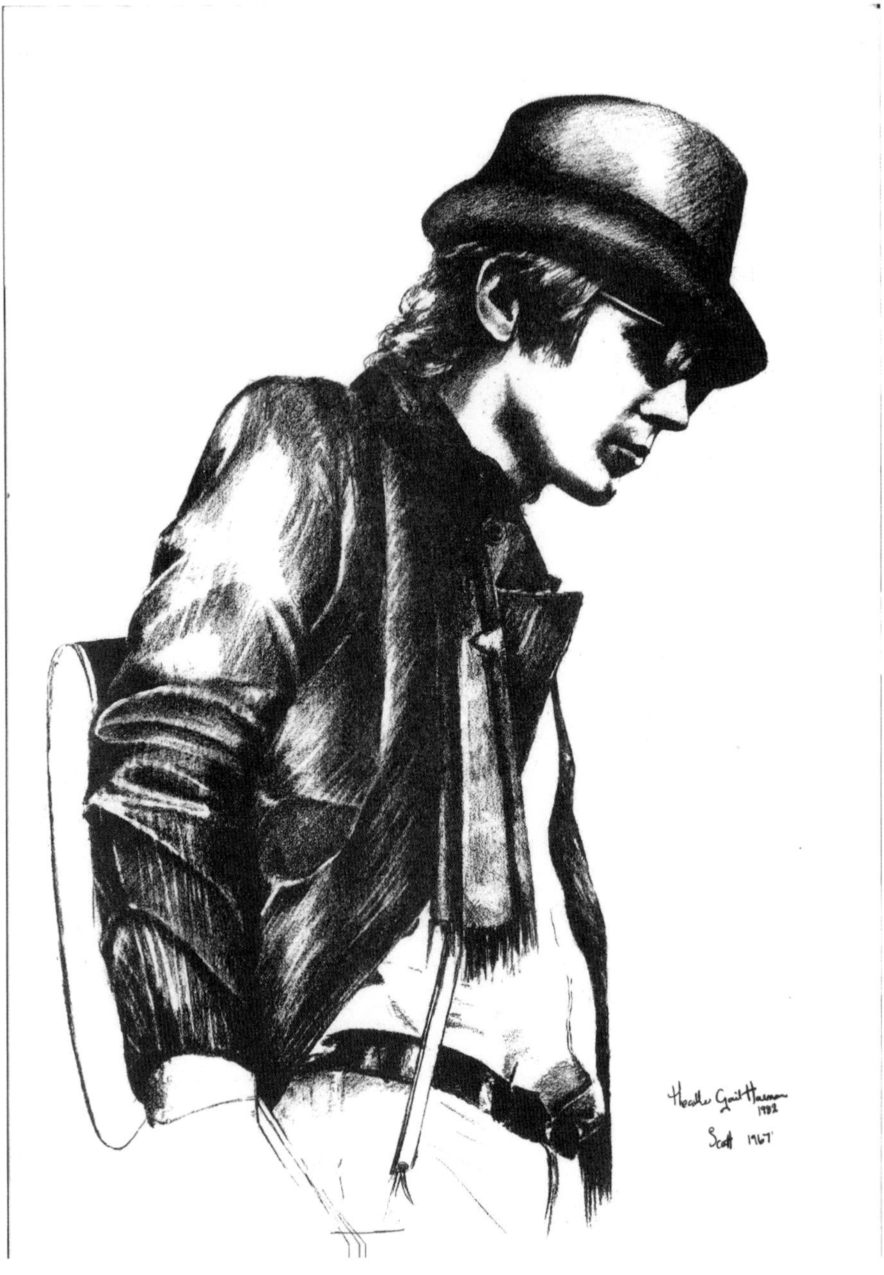
1982
Scott 1967'

Heather Gail Hansen
1982
Scott

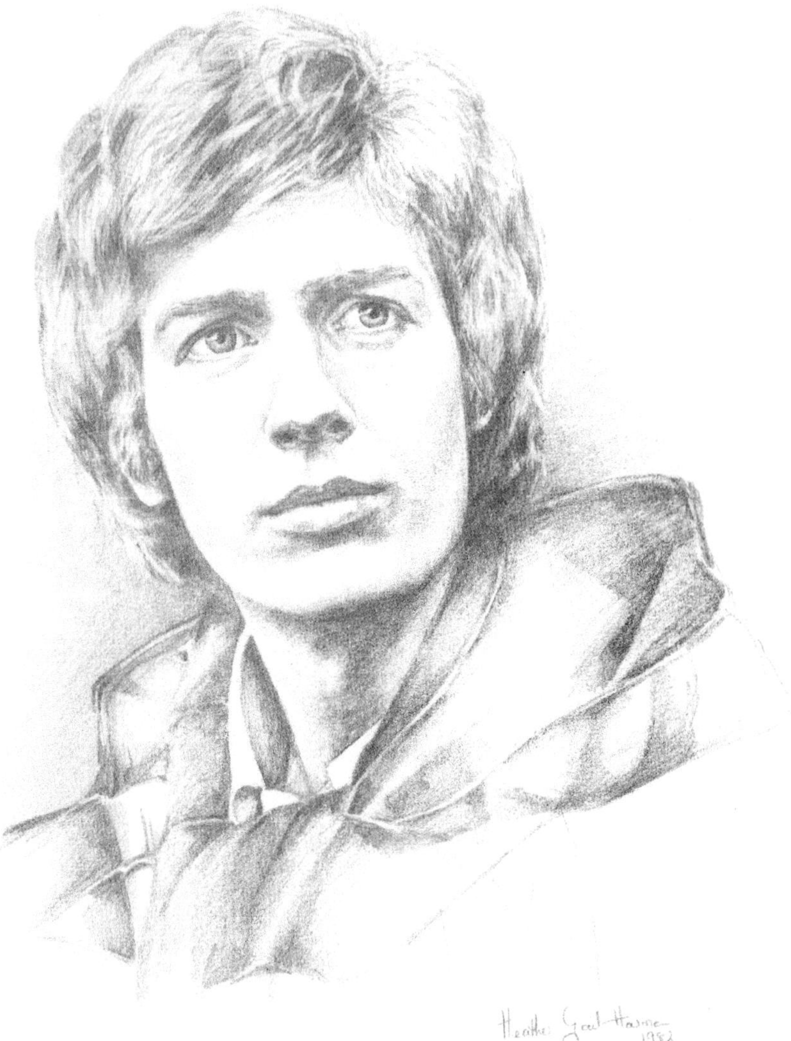
1982

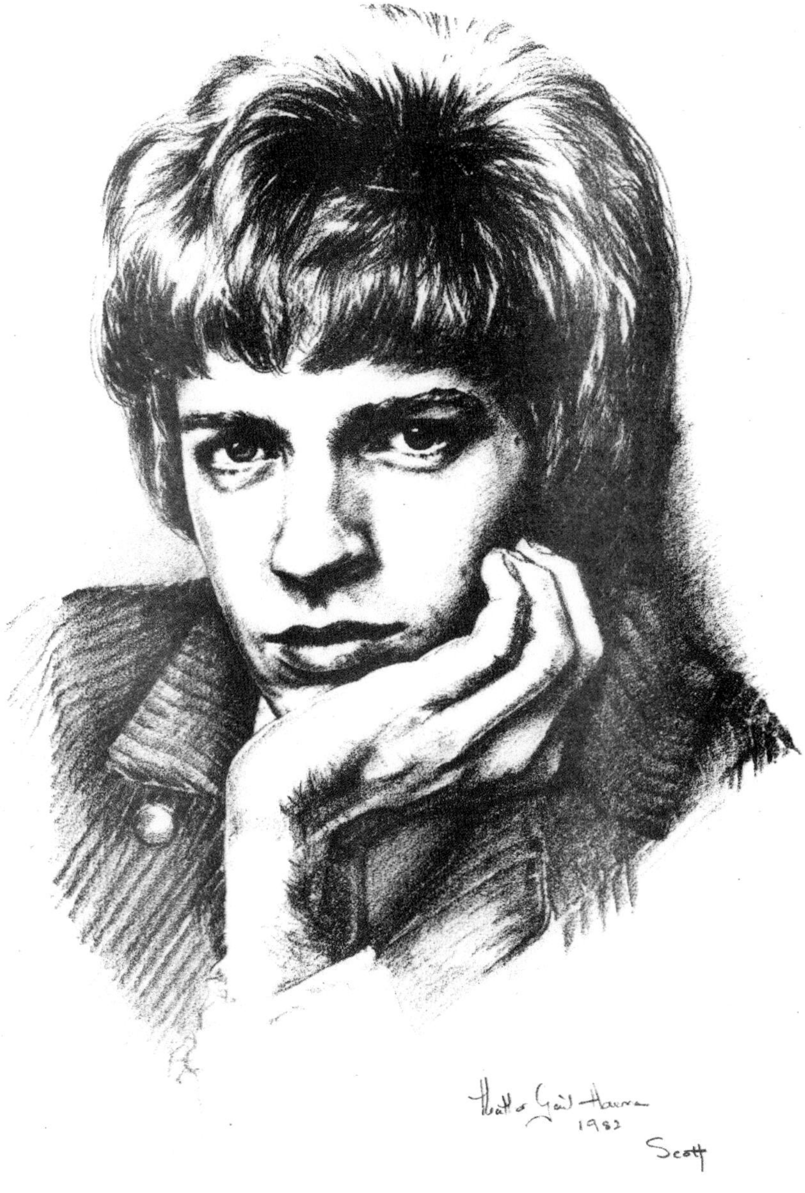
1982
Scott

Lynne Goodall and Alison Wier with triple portrait drawing of Walker Brothers 1980 (now signed by Scott) At the Walker Brothers Convention in London

Scott portrait in process - property of Lynne Goodall. From the Britvic Orange advert photo shoot.

SO CAREER NUMBER TWO BEGAN

MY FIRST ONE WOMAN SHOW IN THE NORTH OF ENGLAND

So I began working on a collection of work which I had been planning for some time. A portrait collection of the great musical names—songwriters. Singer songwriters, musicians. Among them were Michel le Grand and Randy Newman— (Who I discovered through Scott of course), Joni Mitchell, Dylan, Leonard Cohen, Paul Simon, Carol King, Cat Stephens, Neil Diamond, 36 portraits in all—the great singer songwriters.

To do this I needed the help of the recording companies who supplied me with the photography to complete the work and they were very happy to deal with me and saw me as a promotional tool; free advertising etc. I got to know most of the press offices in most of the companies in the 70's and 80's, in the UK and USA.

The exhibition went up in the Preston Guidhall in 1975 and remained there in various forms for 8/9 years. A few sold (my Elton John was stolen!). Eventually other subjects went up as others were sold.

But no Scott. I never painted him in that show for good reason.

I didn't want anyone to make comparisons back then between his career and those of the other big names I was portraying. I didn't want to make those comparisons either.

I was totally unfazed by ringing up the press and arranging interviews and press coverage. My father watched bemused. That is where he thought I would need him once again. I didn't. I wanted him to stay with his writing. Everything worked that way. Probably at that time I became a control freak!

I was making headway and gained some great commissions and contracts from people in the music industry. I even had a social life in the Night clubs in Blackpool.

No Regrets?

In 1975 it happened. Scott had re-joined the Walker Brothers with John and Gary. They had a massive hit with 'No Regrets'. I remember my mother crying when she saw them on TV again, looking great it has to be said and sounding great too. I was transfixed. I had shivers down my spine too, but all I could think about was;

'What has happened? What has gone wrong? 'Why is he doing this?'

My mother was more thrilled than I was for sure she was over the moon. First thing she said was she was looking forward to them touring up north 'so we can go see them!'. (She meant

John!) Oh dear, I thought I didn't like it. They were on TV quite a bit back then, The Vera Lynn Show, Marc Bolan Show, and yes, countless gigs around the country.

Most of my friends in Blackpool were in the entertainments/music world. A couple in particular who were popular female singers around the Northern Club scene. I would sometimes accompany them around the clubs when Will was working in the Leisure industry in Blackpool, literally all hours. It was announced that the Walker Brothers were going to be appearing for one week over in popular cabaret club, Fagins in Manchester. Whilst over there while my friend sang, Jack Diamond, the MC at Fagins (who was an old acquaintance from Blackpool) said, 'Hey we have the Walker Brothers on next weekend are you two coming over?' I knew a lot of people who would be going. My friend Karry said hey Heather you must! You met these guys a few years ago! Yep I certainly did.

I was 'uncomfortable'. No other word to explain it. I just didn't want to go.

I knew Mum and Dad would want to go. John would have been pleased to see them. So I didn't let them know about the Fagins gigs. I remember talking to Will about it (I never talked much about my earlier 'career' to my friends) and he wasn't surprised that I had no intention of going. He thought I might turn up have a few drinks and say something to Scott, because Will knew that I really cared about what was happening. I would have had no right to say anything to Scott. No right at all. I knew that too.

Never once, have I since regretted that decision, not to go to see The Walker Brothers in the 70's. I would not have been able to look him in the eyes. I didn't agree on any level on what he was doing, and also knowing full well that given a free choice and opportunity he would have chosen his own path, and this wasn't it. I imagined that he would have been smashed much of the time and I didn't want to see that either.

On the other hand, I also didn't begrudge John and Gary getting the group back. Getting anyone to understand my feelings in the 70's would have been difficult, so I rarely, if ever, spoke about it. One thing I knew, If Scott had remembered me, he might even have been interested to know how well I was doing, and what I was doing; basically had I got to college? It just wasn't a comfortable situation. People in Fagins knew me as a successful artist. Little realising that not going to college is something I regretted. Not one of my friends knew about how I started in art and about the role Scott played in it all.

If I had have asked him anything it would have been what went wrong? Although but that time his interviews in the music press pointed a finger firmly at his prior record company CBS. I had a few friends in CBS who loved to send me photos of the acts on their rosta to paint. I remember asking a woman I had a lot of phone calls with Ellie Smith, what has happened with Scott Walker? No comment was the loud reply.

What would I have been able to say to Scott?

How are you doing? Glad to see you back with the group? Well I wasn't.

'Thanks to you I was able to find the strength to appreciate my own creativity and fight my corner to protect my right to be my own artist; not as great an artist as you but working at being the best I can be.'

Would he have appreciated that then? No. I tend to think 'thinking' along those lines was something he probably avoided as much as possible at the time and definitely not at the bar after a Walker Brothers show, when getting smashed was probably the important thing to do. It would have been for me in his shoes.

I remember writing to the MD of GTO at some point, Dick Leahy a charming man and clearly a 'fan' of the group and/or Scott. I explained my work and it seemed he had heard of me via the Preston Guildhall exhibition. A few of his acts appeared there. He was so helpful and offered any number of photos of the band for my use for artwork. When I saw the 'Lines' album cover I regretted not taking him up on that offer. I did pass up on producing work of the band for exhibition although I had many photos sent. If you had asked me then why I didn't want to produce work of them I would not have been able to tell you.

So they had two albums as the reformed Walker Brothers;

Then Came Nite Flights

Was Scott really 'free' at last? This was the creative Scott; the artist.

Scott the artist was still there. The magnificent 'Electrician', showing his brilliance. The big question when it was released was what would happen next? Scott had 'escaped' again and how? What next? The Nite Flights album, was a pretty strange collection of John and Gary's work as well as Scott's and clearly they had been given the brief to just go for it. Well they did just that. So Dick Leahy had given Scott his head? He was a fan yes, but to give John and Gary the same freedom? Wow. Why? Well, GTO didn't survive much longer.

To Scott Engel fans it was a time of hope in the face of great despondency. Scott's new work was no more 'commercially marketable' than Scott 4; as brilliant as it was artistically, it was not' commercial'. What would happen was anyone's guess, but in the midst of the disco era, I for one was not too hopeful.

More than that was it to be taken seriously? I mean it was a Walker Brothers album, not a Scott album. There seemed to be more questions than answers. The big one being whoever gave them the go ahead for that would seemed to have been committing commercial suicide. Unless GTO knew it was going under anyway? In which case all credit to Dick Leahy.

And then there was Nothing—The Dark Years begin

The Preston Exhibition and other exhibitions were keeping me quite busy. By the end of the 70's I had landed myself some great contracts, one being for Billy Connolly, who had seen the Preston Show and wanted me to do a complete selection of work of his entire tour crew, which to be presented to them from him as his tour gifts at the final show of the tour. (It was common for the star to buy gifts for the road and sound crew at the end of a busy tour). It was a hectic period and hilarious too. I was his tour artist. I love that man. I did work for Harvey Goldsmith, the promoter, around then too. He had just taken Elton John and Ray Cooper (the percussionist maestro who also appeared on Scott's albums and one of the music industry's true gentlemen) To Russia, which was big news back then. I completed work of them too. This period was the start of a fruitful time for me, working for many notable names.

But news on the Scott front was scant. After the GTO contract, it seems little was happening. But, the irony is, Nite Flights had bought about a new appreciation for Scott's music. The new game in town was dropping his name at every turn. A game played from Bowie to David Sylvian, Julian Cope and all points in between.

Walkerpeople

So I was still taking the music magazines to see who was touring and whether they were going to the Guildhall, and looking always for anything on Scott. Around about that time I saw a small ad in the back of one of the mags— 'Walkerpeople—and a phone number. It said very little, but I played a hunch and rang the number. And so began a long friendship with Lynne Goodall who produced the Walkerpeople mag until its 100th edition. She was just starting up around that time. We would meet up almost every year in London. The first time being for a Walkerpeople convention in the Kingsley Hotel around 1979/80. A fun event, and Dezo Hoffman the photographer turned up. I found his stories about his clients and contracts in the music industry fascinating and of course remembered so many of the wonderful pics of Scott he took. He bought a lot over with him. Dezo's photography career was amazing.

I can't even imagine how many hours Lynne and I spent on the phone over the years. There were times it would be daily, depending on what was going on or who she was going to meet. On all things 'artist' ring would ask me for an opinion. She spent a lot of time visiting various offices and meeting (over the years) all of Scott's managers. There was David Apps (manager of 70's pop group Mud), then Ed Bicknall (manager of Dire Straits). Then of course Charles Negus Fancy, who is still his manager. She would visit them as often as she could to get any information to put in the newsletter, and in doing so left them with no illusions Walkerpeople was growing and interest was growing too; and not just from the old fans. Normally she would ring me and tell me what happened.

As for news of Scott? Still very little. Lynne hadn't met him at that time. She rang me one morning to say he was going to be at a recording studio where he was producing something for a friend, and I said why don't you go along? For me to go from Blackpool wasn't possible. I had already sent a portrait down to her for her to have made into prints for the newsletter members, so I said to her, take it to the studio and get Scott to sign it. (Completed from some of the photos Dick Leahy had sent me), All went quiet on the phone. ' Do you think he would', she asked? 'What have you got to lose?' I said. A few hours later she rang me in a state of shock to say she had met him and he signed her portrait! She sent me a photo of the signed portrait. Evidently he was his usual polite self, and she was thrilled.

Early 80's and no news until of course news of the Virgin deal eventually filtered through which Lynne had learned of pretty early on.

Maisie van Courtland

At that time I came across Maisie Van Courtland. I had written to her when someone suggested Maisie had mentioned a portrait, and seemed to be describing the one I gave Scott, which she had seen at his mother's house in California. And so began another wonderful friendship with a special lady. Maisie had undertook to keep the Scott Walker Newsletter going.

Maisie was a gem; straight out of Agatha Christie, a lady of advanced years with hat gloves and a stick, and a fascinating life in the London theatre scene. Her role I was never sure of, but she was very well connected. Her family knew Ian Fleming and Noel Coward and she had fond memories of him as a child in the West Indies. As to how she became a champion of Scott and determined to keep his name alive in the 70's I don't know, but I did ask her and basically Maisie had a great regard for Scott's mother and a massive respect for Scott's talent; 'I do it for Betty'. She had at some point been to California and stayed with Betty Engel and knew her family, and met up with Betty when she visited the UK way back too.

At some point she asked me if it would be OK for her (with my help) to write an account of my meeting with Scott, for her 50th edition of the Scott Newsletter. As edited by Maisie, the account is somewhat different to my own perspective, because her agenda was firmly in the idea of the misunderstood Scott; one who was perceived as a 'Monster' (her words not mine); and this was a point of view she was keen to refute. Her reasoning at the time was around the idea that Scott was without a recording contract, and this was probably because everyone in the music industry misunderstood him and considered him difficult to work with. For some reason she considered my meeting with him, ' artist to artist', as a story which showed that he was indeed very human and not a 'Monster'.

She was a lady with many friends and was widely respected, and getting to know her I can understand why. We corresponded for many years, she would meet me on my London visits, and she loved to see my daughter Deborah and knowing she was a fan of the band The Police, she would bring Debs photos of them. I had confided in Maisie about my early issue with my father, who was at that point happily writing up a storm. She loved to learn about my relationship with my complex, but clever, father. I would hear about how Betty was and the California family. I remember she knew Jack Leeds too (Gary's father). She would also tell me her opinion of his managers and they came and went, (with great humour!)

Maisie adopted Betty's term of endearment for Scott 'Young Sir', and that is what we called him too. At Christmas she looked forward to her card from Scott 'in his wonderful shaky scrawl' She genuinely worried for Scott and his future. A lot of us did, but Maisie was a mother hen where Scott was concerned. (We finally established that the portrait Betty had was not the one I did for Scott.)

I thought a great deal of Maisie, a true British eccentric with enormous integrity, and I eventually gave her 4 portrait drawings of Scott for her to have printed or at least run a competition to win one in the Newsletter. (A couple of years ago a lady contacted me to tell me she was one of the winners! If anyone reading this has one of them—please get in touch!) Maisie would send me photos of Scott as a baby, a toddler, all through the years in fact. And stories of his childhood career (from Betty). Maisie and Betty were much of the same age I think. She sent me photos of Scott, Mette and baby Lee, and once a message from Betty for me too, about how happy she was to hear of my artistic success. Maisie would also send me exhibition catalogues and art books that she thought I might like.

In 1984 Maisie wrote to me to tell me that an old friend of Scott was very interested in having a portrait of Scott painted by me, and she wanted my permission to set up a meeting when I was next in London.

'You might have come across him Heather. His name is Ralph Gurnett?'

Indeed I had heard of Ralph, and as far as I could then remember, we had in fact met before. Ralph had worked originally in Capable Management, the Walker Brothers management company, and later became Scott's Personal Assistant of sorts. So we met in the Regent Palace Hotel lounge bar; Maisie, Ralph and myself. A great afternoon of stories and laughs, Ralph's reminiscences, and his obvious respect, regard and affection for Scott, made for a real interesting afternoon! He said he had been on a flight recently with Bowie, and they met up in the airport bar where David told him that he wanted to see Scott back working and would help if he could. We discussed the fact that there was a lot of interest in Scott (this would have been around 1985) We did finally get round to talking about the proposed portrait.

I have fond memories of Maisie for sure. Such a caring and clever lady, who also did her bit to make sure that Scott's management knew there was still massive interest in his career.

A Meeting which I can't forget

One of my exhibits at the Guildhall in Preston was of Michel Legrand, the massively talented French Composer, who had been a child musical protege. I was introduced to his music through Scott, who had recorded Legrand songs on the Walker Brothers albums. So when the opportunity arose and Michel was to appear in the Blackburn King Georges Hall, with his Jazz ensemble of four greatly respected musicians, the manager of the Guildhall in Preston where my exhibition was arranged that I could go back stage in Blackburn and ask him to sign my work up sketches of the portrait I produced. By that time I had quite a collection or personally signed work. (Which I still have).

So the meeting was to be between his two shows at Blackburn.

Legrand was not exactly a 'star' on tour with a massive popular following. But the Hall was packed with clearly enthusiastic fans. But, my husband Will remembers that meeting, and wickedly reminds me of it often. We both had met many big names by this point and I had little 'fear' in going backstage to have Michel sign my work. So what happened when he walked into his dressing room, with his slight paunch and smoking a pipe, took me by surprise.

Maybe it was his French accent, or his disarming charm and friendly manner. Maybe it was being in the presence of a massive musical talent, or his confidence, but he spoke to me and I froze. I had lost my power of speech, and I turned into a coy shy 5 year old! I told him eventually I was a fan of his music and had been for many years. Now I was not that old and he asked me how I would have known about his music as a teenager?' because of Scott Walker' I said. We finally talked of Scott. How he once said Once Upon as Summertime was 'the most beautiful song ever written'. He clearly knew some of the work Scott had done with his music. I told him that I wished Scott had sang 'Pieced of Dreams'. He loved one of my portraits:

'Can I have it?' I was taken by surprise. 'Yes, of course.' I said.

He asked me to dedicate it to him and he did the same on the remaining one for me.

To this day I remember how strange it was that I reacted as I did in his presence and not in the presence of others or Scott? But I did, and much to the amusement of husband Will! I think it was because I knew I was in the presence of musical royalty; and a massive talent. That has always impressed me and probably always will.

A Waiting Game

And throughout all of this was a genuine despair about what was happening with Scott. It was annoying. After Nite Flights (and the increased mentions of him from anyone with musical taste in the music press) I had hopes. Julian Cope's release of 'The Godlike Genius of Scott Walker' was pretty reflective of some of the reports I was hearing re a resurgence of interest in Scott Walker. Having a few friends in the Music industry myself by that time, I would hear his name was being dropped left right and centre by a variety of people. I remember picking up my copy of new Musical Express to see a picture that could have been Scott—it was in fact a profile of up and coming David Sylvian and the article laced with references to Scott. It started to be a fun game. I ended up keeping a list of the of people who mentioned Scott in the music press like it was some kind of currency or measure of authenticity and meanwhile no one was signing him. The frustration was real. What must it have been like for him?

In short whilst he wasn't in charge of his artistic freedom, there was something pretty wrong in my world. And both Maisie and Lynn felt that way too. I admired the way both of them would put themselves out to visit anyone who could give them any news about Scott, good news preferably but in fact any news at all, knowing as they did that it helped to get the message across that he still had an audience and they were waiting. They never met however. I used to tell both of them that the music industry might be buzzing with his name again, but that their constant visits to managers offices, and record companies etc. were valuable because they left no doubt that the old fans were there and that new fans were growing. That is important market research.

As Scott would say 'it is a waiting game.' And he sure perfected it! If there was a Lifetime Achievement award for waiting it out he would win outright.

But then so did some of us play the waiting game, knowing that kind of creative original talent could not be ignored forever.

When planning to write this account, I dug out some old files and correspondence. And I began to look at it with fresh eyes, having not seen it for some time. People today often want to know how I know so much about Scott's career? Well the answers are both within this narrative and in the fact that Lynne Goodall produced a true historical chronicle from 1980 (?) until 2006.

It was difficult to put together a Newsletter on a regular basis when news was so thin on the ground. But Lynne managed to find just about every article every written or as they were written all over Europe and the US. Japan and wherever any one was interviewing Scott she managed to get hold of the transcript, sometimes curtesy of his management who would know when interviews were planned. Same with photo shoots. She also kept up a comprehensive coverage of all available

Walker Brothers and Scott records.

When news was not on the cards Lynne would publish chosen articles from the archives. But in truth, much of the 'news' was keeping an eye on whoever it was in the music press who was mentioning Scott that week.

Lynne rang me quite surprised one day to find that Scott was to go back to art college. A great college too, and I can well understand it was something he wanted to do and whilst action on the music scene was thin on the ground, I suppose he thought 'why not'? I was also a little jealous! My guess is a few people knew where he was daily but hopefully no one spoilt it for him, certainly Lynne at Walkerpeople didn't advertise his venture into art college, and he had work in the degree show along with all the other students. She took photos of those which I also have.

I remember our thoughts when CD's first emerged. Back then there was some measure of respect when an artist had their work put on CD; totally the opposite today of course; Kudos is for having your work released on vinyl. To get Scott on CD was an exciting time. It was a sign that he was being taken seriously even though not working at that time. To be honest there were times the idea of Scott on CD seemed unlikely.

When there was any action on the Scott front Lynne new about it. There was a network of sorts and not forgetting much of this before the internet, but throughout the lean years of the 80's (not including the Climate of Hunter period), the network slowly grew. And eventually a new era of fans came through and we would talk about this a lot. I would say to her, that all the efforts she was putting in would not be wasted if a new wave of fans emerged. Walkerpeople grew too. And I think Lynne would agree if I said that is when all of the effort started to be rewarded. It was not totally dedicated to Scott of course and articles about John and Gary were never missed. I think Lynn was the first to know when Gary started producing his sandcastles. Also when John was due to visit from the USA. She would go to meet him in London.

And then came more … … … … Waiting.

For me the 80's were exciting times. I completed a very large oil painting of Elton John to raise funds for the Olympic Appeal Fund and it was duly taken down to Watford, and Elton had a lot of publicity arranged with him and the painting. I worked with and for many famous names, and completed work for the Preston exhibition, Jasper Carrot, Mike Harding (who I ended up completing a few pieces of work for) Boy George and many more. There were more exhibitions and more commissions.

Come on Down!

At one point I decided I needed to be my own secretary so I took a London Chamber of Commerce Information technology Diploma and learned how to type. Part of passing the Diploma was to apply for an interview for a job placement. Well at that time I had an exhibition up in the North West apart from the Guildhall one. Also had commissions to fulfil. Of course I didn't want or need a 'job', but needs must, so more than a little tongue in cheek I applied for the position as Production

Co-ordinator for the stage show of The Price is Right game show, and Personal Assistant to Leslie Crowther. The show was to come to Blackpool for a full season to the wonderful old Grand Theatre. Out of 300 odd applicants I got the job! So I did it and had a fabulous experience in the production a TV show in a wonderful old theatre and working with some of the most wonderful people. My immediate boss was William G Stewart, he of game show '15 to 1' fame. He was the Producer of the Price is Right.

My employer however was the legendary Billy Marsh, entertainments impresario, and CEO of London Management; the management body for which virtually everyone with a TV or entertainment career in the UK, were represented by. The big names in power back then were Billy Marsh, Lou Grade, Bernard Delfont. Great times and great memories, and at the end of the season contract Billy and Jan Kennedy who was his right hand lady, had already told me that had I been able to move to London, there was a job there for me in Artists management. They even dropped a hint of who I might be managing. (Jan eventually ran London Management on the death of Billy). The truth is Will had a great job which he loved and Deborah was just 14 and had all her major schooling to go through still and I couldn't have taken up that offer. It was interesting to know though that my skills in artists management situations had been noticed. I was told that one of the reason I got the job is that I was comfortable in back stage situations and I was used to meeting big name artists! Well that was true. Needless to say I ended up completing a number of portraits, of Leslie Crowther, Gary Wilmot and others who were all part of the show.

Creativity of a different kind — My Inspiration and the Football Association National Exhibition.

I had never actually had a 'job' in the real sense (based on my new qualifications) and it had proved a great experience. So when offered the chance to transfer my skills into the world of football, well to be honest it wasn't my thing. But the work interested me. And it was short term. I liked to dabble in work in the short term! I ended up doing a short term based at Blackpool FC and my main contribution was fund raising. The football club was in financial trouble and within 10 weeks I had set up a fun run and bought in sponsors to cover all costs. It earned around £14,000. So Sponsorship became one of my prized skills.

I was also on the committee of the Club's Centenary celebrations and managed with great difficulty to 'sell' the idea of an exhibition in an art gallery for their centenary launch. No one wanted to know. Art and Football would never meet. There was a lot of resistance — who would want to go to a museum to see an exhibit about football? Well I had seen what exhibits the club had hidden away in the south stand attic! Amazing pictures and group photos going back 100 years. It is amazing what people cannot see when they live amongst it. So I ended up fighting both the club, and believe it or not my friends at the local Gallery/museum (where I have exhibited over the years) who were equally as resistant to the idea of football memorabilia going on their walls! I eventually got the event going even if it was like pulling teeth! The only way I did it was because it wasn't going to cost the club anything and I was bringing in the old BFC famous names to play a part in the event.

I was right of course. It was a massive success. The BBC covered the event! Everyone was there. The following year Preston council took my idea and opened a Football Association Football exhibition. It is now permanently homed in Manchester. My idea from front to back and boy did it take some convincing to get it going. It took an artist with a good eye for marketing and promotion, and an eye to sponsorship opportunities, plus a mass of experience in putting on art exhibitions to even imagine it. Pretty rare qualifications. You don't get many of them in football. As to whether I will ever be given the 'official' credit for that is another matter. Football is a man's world still.

Spreading my Creative Wings

I found myself in a strange position where my skills in large events sponsorship were much valued. I found it a really creative exercise. I loved seeing a plan coming together. It was great satisfying and for charities in particular it was very really valuable. So at home armed with my contact list (the most treasured possession in sponsorship circles) I raised funds for Bernardo's children's charity and made a massive headway into my pet project, starting a feasibility study for a new museum for the Leisure Industry — I lived in a museum called Blackpool. Having not grown up there I saw it for what it was — a totally unique museum to the leisure and holidaymaking culture with Victorian purpose built palaces dedicated to leisure. To this day if someone tries to open such a museum in the UK I am the list to be contacted. It I all on file in the UK heritage and museums commission.

So my life was not exactly locked up in an attic painting all day.

A Teaching Opportunity

At the same time Scott went to art college, I was asked by my local education authority if I would consider teaching at my local college (the last art teacher having died suddenly). Would I step in? Well I had no real intention of teaching until much older but I went along to talk about it and accepted the contract. Again only for a few hours a week so I was happy with that.

That was a moment that truly did impact on my life. I took full teacher training at the same time as taking my first classes of students.

I found I loved teaching, and mentoring and do to this day, and as much as I love to be behind my easel, I love to teach, and that too has given me an extraordinary career. As a teacher I have had some fabulous experiences. Will and I have taken countless groups on painting holidays abroad, and worked regularly in the residential colleges in the UK; specialist weeks dedicated to portraiture which attracted students from as far away as South Africa and the USA. So for much of the year we were working in fabulous British Heritage country houses.

And for Scott—more waiting.

Whilst Scott was at college there was little news on the recording front of course. But had there been, Lynne would have heard about it. The Walkerpeople network had grown and a substantial amount of members were not 'old fans'. There was a mass of new interest in the music of Scott Walker. So much of the content of her newsletter was in highlighting all the new interest; not just mentioning Scott, but accredited with being the inspiration behind so many respected new artists.

And along came Serendipity.

My card from Gary

Scott was at art college and I had in my hand a letter written by him. He was thanking Lynne Goodall for not letting his whereabouts of the art school be known to Walkerpeople, but she sent me a copy because in the letter he talked of an artist who he loved and Lynne could not recognise the name; partly because she might not have heard of this artist and partly because it was difficult to read his handwriting.

To say that Scott's handwriting is idiosyncratic is an understatement. He would have made a great doctor (UK joke). So for a moment I stopped reading in my tracks. I was looking at the handwriting. Where had I seen that before? I searched for my postcard from Gary. Within 10 seconds it was plainly obvious. My card had been sent from Scott, not Gary. Oh boy. I rang Lynne, and I remember saying;

'Lynne, you won't believe this. My card from Gary was written by Scott.'

'You're joking.

'No doubt. This is the handwriting, you can hardy mistake it.'

How did I now know? Why didn't I have any idea (Doh No!) Was I sure? Oh definitely.

But as the conversation went on all became transparently clear. The words on the card now made sense. Above all else I remember thinking 'How Dumb had I been not to realise?' Well the answer to that was also understandable. At that time I still thought it was from Gary because of the 'Pet' reference, even though I couldn't understand why Gary would have written what it said. We had spent a long time that afternoon holed up in the back room of a record shop. We chatted about a lot of stuff. Gary would have said something like 'Hey, I remember these portraits! Great you are in the Daily Mirror! Congratulations!

So one day in August in London, there was a copy of the Daily Mirror and Gary said Hey that is her, 'Pet' Heather! (Having met me only a couple of weeks before in the Disci record shop. Gary and Scott shared a flat in Chiswick at that time)

He wrote:

Chiswick W4, Ron Kiss, 16/8/66

Dear Pet Heather

'This publicity will put you on top. Your drawings are the most excellent I seen. This will give you <u>the chance</u> the <u>artist wants</u>!'

The truth is had it not been for 'Pet' Heather, I would probably not have given the card a second look; but understandably I still thought it must have been from Gary. It was enough for me that Gary should have bothered to write to me back then.

But he had dropped all the hints that most fans would have recognised. The 'Ron Kiss' was a name often used by the group. (In fact it was mentioned in the questionnaire completed by the group in the Rave magazine in 66.) It would seem Scott expected me to know who had sent it. What kind of fan was I!?

So I in turn sent a copy of my card down to Lynn. She rang me when she got it. WOW! How would you have felt had you have known back then? Scott writing to fans was never heard of. Well put it this way thanks to publicist Dad the local press ran the story of my getting a card from Gary on the front page! Had it been known it was from Scott, one can only imagine!

So was it a cool story she could put into Walkerpeople? I don't think either of us discussed that option. Why?

He was and remains the subject of massive artistic respect. The Godlike Genius of Scott Walker was and is a growing legend. All focus was on the next album, and whether it would materialise, and the message in the card would probably have had many in his new fan base scratching their heads in puzzlement.

Above all Scott was 'cooool'. Even at the core of his 60's career was the massive achievement of him being considered a serious artist, in a pop music world that never expected that of their stars. Having been Little Scotty Engel would most likely not have been seen as 'cool'. So not knowing at the time about his early years as a teenage star, the words to me at the time would have seemed bizarre, if I had realised it was from him. Really bizarre. What a totally different attitude from his renowned love of privacy, the usual Scott Walker? The press's favourite 'Garbo' persona? The reclusive misfit artist in search of a creative destiny who clearly wasn't a fan of publicity as a means to artistic freedom; *especially as a way to achieve artistic excellence.*

Having a young teenage career is something most people have no idea about. I did, and I guess he identified that. It is real complicated. Scott knew what it was like to negotiate a way through childhood when you have a talent and he didn't only reach out he opened up. But the irony is he still would not have wanted his childhood/teenage career made known in the UK. He wrote a message to me wearing a private hat that he wanted no one to know about back then.

My Dad had suffered a heart attack in the 80's, and I went to see him with the letter and the card but before showing them to him I said,

'Dad you remember that card I got from Gary? The pet Heather one?'—guess who actually sent it?

'Scott' he said without pause.

'What made you think that?

'Because it was either him or Gary; you told me they lived together and it wasn't Gary who wrote that card.' He said.

'That and the fact that you got in to meet him at Coventry'.

When Dave Adams from the daily Sketch had 'arranged' the meeting, it was in the proviso there was no publicity. There was a noticeable 'welcome', in that dressing room; Scott was happy enough to meet me. As Dad said 'Or you would most definitely not have been taken into the wings to watch the show. Maurice was 'put out'. He said Scott never took anyone to the wings.'

OK. Well that had occurred to me. It surprised me at the time. On thinking about it Ronnie Scott didn't expect me in the wings either; as polite and nice as he was. A surreal moment to be honest.

More Serendipity

But that was not all the story. It seems that in the biggest paper in the UK back then, The Daily Mirror, my story busted another story. A story that worried many Scott fans. How big the Mirror was meant to make that story I will never know but I can guess. Scott being pulled out of a gas filled flat. It was reported the same day as my page three coverage; in a tiny sentence or two on a different page. (Hence my phone call to Brian Sommerville's office—and being put through to him.) No wonder the Mirror guys wanted us in the Town Hall in Rugby at 10.30pm with the Mayor. No wonder their comments about 'beats the 'other story'. It surprised us at the time that my little portrait story was so 'urgent'.

Scott was probably expecting the worst when he picked up the

Daily Mirror. As it was my story must have been manna from heaven. And that was probably reason enough for him to send that card.

Going through everything he was experiencing, he still found time, no matter what state his head was in, to reach out and make sure as best he could that I got that card.

As for the contents of the card, well back in the 60's it would have been news: but in the 80's, yes there were people who would have loved to know the story, *but* many of the new fans having emerged with the Godlike Genius of Scott Walker album (Julian Cope) in their collections, Scott was, and is, quite rightly revered for his artistic integrity. He was a real icon and now even more so, having past his seventieth year. A musical genius who followed his own creative path and the sentiment in that card would have been a dichotomy too far for the more sensitive souls! Oh don't you just love the irony though?

So after all the story so far, when I found out the truth about my card, when I sat back and thought about it, my respect for Scott Engel went through the roof. I was no longer fourteen, fifteen, sixteen; I was in my late 30's. I had been through a lot myself by that time.

I remember Lynne and I talking about the ins and outs of it all back then and both smiling at the irony. His newly acquired fan base; what would they have made of that card? For him to do that for a 'fan' who had a talent, respect to you Scott. Under the circumstances at that time, to have had the generosity of spirit to consider sending me a such card was astonishing.

So what were the 90's to add to the story?

My life was to be turned upside down in 1989. Will was forced to leave his much loved job due to disability and Deborah was due to go to University. I remember ringing her to tell her that not only was she going to university, both her Mother and Father were going too! Was she surprised? I doubt it. By that time very little I did surprised her. In September 1990 Will and I entered Lancaster university and Deborah to UCL in London. Will was still young and needed a new focus and I had always wanted to back track into learning. So at the same time as teaching I was in university studying the history of my medium. (Pastel — and the creative development of women in the 19th century. Women artists in particular.)

Three years later, Debs and I received our First class honours degrees on the same day! Will still had a year to go.

My career since has gone from strength to strength; not least of all because Will and I were now a team. Without him I could not have done what I did. We had a great time.

My creativity is totally in my own control and I create what I want when I want. I have collectors of my work which is a great position to be in. I now teach, and mentor, I write for at magazines and for many years travelled everywhere with great groups of people all enjoying their painting holidays and courses. I'm lucky enough now to be regarded an authority in my medium and I have recently launched a brand new online teaching venture. I exhibit in the National Pastel Society shows as regularly as I can and also in China and Taiwan.

For Scott the 90's meant more and more waiting until what is widely regarded as a breakthrough album 'Tilt'. In so many ways the album was what a new generation of Scott fans were waiting for, and many of the old ones too. Other albums have followed, and each one consolidating his position as both an iconic and current musical force. And that is the point; he now has what seems to be as close to pure artistic freedom as he will ever be, and whilst that situation remains, all is well with my world. But it was a long time coming.

In 2004 Will and I moved to the mountains of Spain, to build our home as a great place to paint and where I have the best times developing my Mediterranean garden which overlooks a view that still takes my breath away. Gardening is like painting to me. I have a great studio and two great dogs who run around the Spanish campo like spring lambs, and a vociferous cat. We are surrounded by wildlife; eagles fly outside our lounge window, and goats across the top of our drive, and chameleons 'jive' across our terrace.

Scott has, at long last, his artistic freedom. His work is now out there; not only on CD but now the kudos is finding his original albums on vinyl! And even on new vinyl pressings. his work is now valued as it should be. Hopefully he calls the shots, totally and completely. I know that the one thing I value above everything after my family is my artistic integrity and creative freedom.

And I know the extent to which I owe that to one man. Scott was my muse, my inspiration, my idol and a good part of my teenage education. That he wrote to me at a time when things were not as good as they could have been for him, and made my meeting with him a treasured memory, is something that I cannot thank him enough for. Meeting your idol is always a risk.

I have never told this story before, although there have been a few who said I should write about my life, very few will have had an idea of this story. One way or another, tying the threads together has not been an easy task. But my reason for writing it has never been in question.

Artistic freedom — it is all about artistic freedom and about the business that is whatever a young talent, an artist, has to negotiate to be able to function in a creative sense; especially since in all too many cases the guys that pull the strings are the guys that make the money. It's the same in the Fine art/painting world. The galleries and the agents call the shots. In Scott's case 'the music industry'. Notorious in every sense as a money making machine. He learned early on that 'Fame' was transient. But talent wasn't. Talent would prevail. Talent could open doors. He had proved it with the Walker Brothers. He had more than proved it with his solo 60's career. And he is proving it again now.

There isn't a greater Blueprint for an artist out there. And for that single fact I have spent much of my life being grateful.

POSTSCRIPT

This story was completed in late 2016. Developments in my life, but more importantly in Scott's career made me hold off for a few months. I think my motivation to get the story written at all has been some of my friends on Scott's Facebook groups; the one I admin is The Scott Walker Fan Club which says it all I suppose but not my choice of name. It has been exciting to see the massive new interest in him and his career. The SWFC is a strange beast in fact, it has members who go back as far as I do and others who are in their early 20's! Conversations tend to fall into two distinct camps but it seems to work.

The internet has made it so much easier to keep track on what is happening in Scott's career. So now it is fun to see new fans who are also becoming aficionados of Scott Engel. Whereas we used to depend on the music press, now Google does a far more comprehensive job of keeping records available.

But I held back from publishing this last year on hearing that Scott was to be honoured with a night at the Proms in his name. I cannot begin to say what that meant to me. I can't even find the words now easily.

Over the years thanks to Lynn, and her contacts, I have heard so many of Scott's interviews in Europe with various journalists. We saw the Scott on the Tube back in the early 80's, and various BBC interviews, frankly sounding tentative and often defensive. Always a little 'guarded', and often I guess fulfilling his record company's commitments. But then I heard Scott's interview with Jarvis Cocker for the BBC. For the first time in years I heard the Scott I had met. On top of his game. The creative artist in his own space, and he seemed really comfortable. I'm welling up as I write this. I get emotional about it. But the other reason I held back from getting this story out is one I didn't really understand.

A couple of years ago I started a new painting of Scott. The first since the one I gave him in 1968. (I did a few drawings for Maisie and one for Lynn but that was it). For whatever reason I couldn't finish it. I then started a couple of paintings of Scott with John and Gary; I couldn't complete them either. So, I have a studio with half a dozen almost completed painting, but the big one, the one of Scott is special. I arranged copyright to use the original image and have developed something that says it all for me.

It was the announcement of the Proms and Jarvis's interview has allowed me to finish it finally. My Scott is back. And creating on his terms. So, I am currently organising the printing of it and it is for the fans. And especially for those who have played an important part in his life. The prints will then go first to the Scott Walker Fan Clubs on Facebook, and a couple of other Facebook Walker Brothers groups on Facebook. Proceeds of those to my rescue dog charities in Spain when I have finished paying the printers etc.

What matters to me is that all of his fans, whether original fans or new ones appreciate this image.

And then for me maybe I will finish the Walker Brothers paintings and I know where some of those must go too. In my mind I can see them finished. Not least of all to Gary and family, who gave me my nickname back in 1966! Pet Heather!

Then for me the circle will be completed. Scott started it and his current success has completed it. Artistic creativity is a journey, sometimes a painful one but rewarding nevertheless. He taught me that. Pragmatism is the key. It can be all a waiting game. That journey moves us forward, which is why I have always understood why he never listens to his work when it is done, it is complete. But to this day it puzzles people why he doesn't listen to his own past music. I don't know a visual artist who constantly revisit their own past work (unless for a learning purpose). What is to be gained from it? What is important to me, and excites me, is the next painting not staring at ones I have already done. How many authors read their own books once they are published? How many directors watch their own movies?

I only hope that other artists might read this. I have tried to make my journey clear to understand. Not all artists will have an inspiration, a muse, an influence as I did. But when you do it is special.

So are artists born, not made?

I was born in my Grandmother's footprint for sure. She was my guiding light and taught me how to live a life of creativity I share her passion especially for music and those great creators of music. But that influence alone would not have seen me through and bought me through. I was as much made by another artist as born one.

And I know that many who read this, even Bowie if he were still with us, Elton for sure, all the greats have had an open heart to magnificent influences that fire them and inspire them. All the great names are fans. As I write this, that is what I am, and always was.

So was Scott, and look what that has given us.

> *I have had a career which has crossed paths for years with many famous names. A few people have said to me that although it is great that I am putting this story out for the 'fans' - it would be interesting if I were to pick up where this book finishes and put another book together on my long and diverse career in art and other areas. So given that Scott was the starting point, I have decided to continue the story, which has been nothing if not unconventional. More than that it is perhaps inspirational to those who are pursuing their own artistic creative career.*
>
> *Any news regarding this will be on my website heatherharmanartist.com. I shall be adding an opt-in for those who want to receive an update re the new publication. Or you can email me at heatherharmanartist@outlook.es.*

ABOUT THE AUTHOR

From the start of her career outlined in this book Heather went on the be the first woman in her medium, pastel, to have her own one woman shows in the north of England from 1975 onwards and subsequently worked with, and for a variety of famous names including musicians, comedians (she was Billy Connolly's Tour artist in 1978/9) and Elton John (for the Olympic Appeal fund in 1976) actors, and then onto theatre TV and sports with so many famous names.

Heather became one of the handful of dedicated tutors of the pastel medium with students on her courses from all over the world; mainly held in the UK between 1989 and 2014, teaching the medium in colleges and private venues all over the UK.

She is now a member or friend of most of the European Pastel Societies and those in the USA and recently became the first woman to be asked to exhibit in the Chinese Pastel Society in 2017 from the UK. She is a popular demonstrator of the medium in the national art societies in Europe and beyond.

She now spends her time in her studio and running her Pastel Academy Online since 2017, teaching artists what she had to learn the hard way without her teenage college education, and writing articles on the medium for magazines since 1995.

Heather was also notably the first professional pastel artist to study the history of the medium in Lancaster University in 1990-4.

Her life's work and beginnings – as this book tells – is condensed into this;

To most artists/creatives in any form; The creative road is rarely a straight or easy path. Many things will throw you off course but stay focused if you can and if not wait. The waiting game is real and a factor in most artists lives. For me the greatest example of this is Scott Walker. I believed he would survive his issues and in fact to me there was no way he couldn't. Why? Because, authentic creative artists have no other choice. He is a true Blueprint for an artist, but he has had to fight his corner.

Every time I think of his trials and creative fights and think of the Proms tribute and I have tingles down my spine. I can cry over that to this day.

Heather lives in the Spanish mountains with her husband and "rock" since her career began in the 60s mentioned in this book.

Printed in Great Britain
by Amazon